THE
EVERYTHING®
Jacqueline Kennedy Onassis Book

Dear Reader,

The image of a shell-shocked Jacqueline Kennedy standing in her bloodstained pink suit next to Lyndon Johnson as he takes the oath of office is forever seared into my memory. Her expression radiates utter loss and grief—as well as a soul-deep dignity.

Jackie's courage in the aftermath of her husband's assassination was nothing short of heroic. Her conduct turned an already popular First Lady into a national icon—and that was the problem. Icons are expected to be perfect, to live up to the ideals the public imposes on them. Jackie refused.

It's ironic that the very qualities that had made her so popular—her devotion to family, her inner strength, her willingness to challenge conventions—would later bring criticism from the public and Kennedy clan alike. But she was determined to live life on her terms.

The goal of this book is to bring the woman behind the legend to three-dimensional life using the remembrances of friends, her own words, and the scholarship of biographers. Its aim is to present Jackie's story within the context of the times, from the roaring twenties to the end of the twentieth century. Jackie's was a life well lived. And perhaps that's her greatest legacy of all.

Kathleen Tracy

Welcome to

THE
EVERYTHING
PROFILES SERIES

Welcome to the EVERYTHING® Profiles line of books—an extension of the bestselling EVERYTHING® series!

These authoritative books help you learn everything you ever wanted to know about the lives, social context, and surrounding historical events of fascinating people who made or influenced history. While reading this EVERYTHING® book you will discover three useful boxes, in additional to numerous quotes:

Fact: *Definitions and additional information*
Question: *Questions and answers for deeper insights*
They Said: *Memorable quotes made by others about this person*

Whether you are learning about a figure for the first time or are just brushing up on your knowledge, EVERYTHING® Profiles help you on your journey toward a greater understanding of the individuals who have shaped and enriched our lives, culture, and history.

When you're done reading, you can finally
say you know **EVERYTHING®**!

DIRECTOR OF INNOVATION Paula Munier

EXECUTIVE EDITOR, SERIES BOOKS Brielle K. Matson

ASSOCIATE COPY CHIEF Sheila Zwiebel

ACQUISITIONS EDITOR Lisa Laing

DEVELOPMENT EDITOR Elizabeth Kassab

PRODUCTION EDITOR Casey Ebert

PHOTO RESEARCHER Robin Gordon

Visit the entire Everything® series at *www.everything.com*

THE

EVERYTHING®

JACQUELINE KENNEDY ONASSIS BOOK

A Portrait of an American Icon

Kathleen Tracy

adamsmedia
avon, massachusetts

An Everything® Series Book.
Everything® and everything.com® are registered
trademarks of F+W Publications, Inc.

Published by Adams Media, an F+W Publications Company
57 Littlefield Street, Avon, MA 02322 U.S.A.
www.adamsmedia.com

ISBN-10: 1-59869-530-4
ISBN-13: 978-1-59869-530-4

Printed in Canada.

J I H G F E D C B A

Library of Congress Cataloging-in-Publication Data
is available from the publisher.

This publication is designed to provide accurate and authoritative information with regard to the subject matter covered. It is sold with the understanding that the publisher is not engaged in rendering legal, accounting, or other professional advice. If legal advice or other expert assistance is required, the services of a competent professional person should be sought.
  —From a *Declaration of Principles* jointly adopted by a Committee of the American Bar Association and a Committee of Publishers and Associations

Many of the designations used by manufacturers and sellers to distinguish their products are claimed as trademarks. Where those designations appear in this book and Adams Media was aware of a trademark claim, the designations have been printed with initial capital letters.

*This book is available at quantity discounts for bulk purchases.
For information, please call 1-800-289-0963.*

Contents

Jacqueline Kennedy Onassis's Ten Most Telling Quotes

1. "The first time you marry for love, the second for money, and the third for companionship."

2. "I don't think there are any men who are faithful to their wives."

3. "I want minimum information given with maximum politeness."

4. "What is sad for women of my generation is that they weren't supposed to work if they had families. What were they going to do when the children are grown—watch the raindrops coming down the window pane?"

5. "I want to live my life, not record it."

6. "When Harvard men say they have graduated from Radcliffe, then we've made it."

7. "There are two kinds of women: those who want power in the world, and those who want power in bed."

8. "If you bungle raising your children, I don't think whatever else you do well matters very much."

9. "The one thing I do not want to be called is First Lady. It sounds like a saddle horse."

10. "Every moment one lives is different from the other. The good, the bad, hardship, the joy, the tragedy, love, and happiness are all interwoven into one single, indescribable whole that is called life. You cannot separate the good from the bad. And perhaps there is no need to do so, either."

Introduction

Jacqueline Kennedy Onassis once said she considered herself a woman first. To her admirers, she is nothing less than an iconic American figure. Over the course of her life, the woman known as Jackie O lived many roles: high society debutante, adventurous professional woman, politician's wife, young mother, First Lady, widow, reluctant public figure, role model, billionaire's wife, dyed-in-the-wool New Yorker, benefactor of the arts, editor, and avid conservationist. But for someone who lived such a public life, she remained an enigma, her carefully polished poise a sometimes impenetrable shield to the woman beneath. Everybody knows of Jackie, but few knew her.

How did an unassuming young woman who dreamed of being a photojournalist become one of the most influential women of the twentieth century, one who forever changed the way we look at the presidency—and ourselves? Part of it was serendipity. At a dinner party thrown by a journalist associate, she happened to meet a young congressman from Massachusetts named John F. Kennedy, who later joked that he'd leaned across the asparagus to ask her out.

Part was opportunistic. Just thirty-one years old when her husband was sworn in as president, Jackie saw an opportunity. She set out to reinvent the public image of the president's wife. She orchestrated a renovation of the White House and invited Americans into her home by hosting a televised tour of the presidential residence. Jackie also became a vocal supporter of the arts, frequently hosting elegant dinner parties that featured some of the most renowned musicians and performers of the day.

Part was fate. During an otherwise unremarkable trip to Dallas, Texas, to drum up Democratic support in a traditionally Republican state, President Kennedy was assassinated. Photographs of a numbed Jackie in her bloodstained suit and her dignified grief turned her into an American symbol of loss, courage, and, ultimately, survival.

Part was calculated. It was no secret that money and financial security were important to Jackie—more important than the approval of the public or the Kennedy clan. After Robert Kennedy's assassination, Jackie's priority became her children's safety. While her marriage to Aristotle Onassis four months later may not have been born from great passion, it provided what Jackie needed: the finances to raise her children in a protected and sheltered environment.

Most of Jackie's legacy came from a unique combination of charisma, intelligence, ambition, and unapologetic determination to live life on her terms. That single-mindedness was greatly influenced by her upbringing: in particular, her close relationship with her charming but roguish father, "Black Jack" Bouvier, which was warm and loving and her cool and emotionally distant relationships with her mother and sister. Hers was a family where appearances often meant everything and the importance of maintaining an appropriate public face was imperative. At the same time, Jackie's parents fostered the independence that led her to pursue an education and career at a time when women were expected to be little more than housewives and mothers.

Even when Jackie was married with children, she refused to disappear into the background, carving out a public persona that overtly promoted the arts and inadvertently made her a fashion trendsetter. Her ability to project deference to her husband's office while remaining a clear partner in their marriage endeared her to people the world over and made her a role model for a generation of young women. President Kennedy once proudly observed that he was becoming best known as the man who married Jackie.

Her popularity may have waxed and waned over the decades, but her influence came to be part of the American fabric. Jackie's lifetime spanned some of the nation's most volatile and transforming eras. Through it all, she transcended the changing social, cultural, and political mores to emerge as the ultimate and enduring symbol of style, class, dignity, and grace under fire. Her story remains timely and her legacy timeless.

Chapter 1

A CHILD OF PRIVILEGE

While the Founding Fathers may have rejected the British monarchy and class system, America has long had its own brand of aristocracy—one based on wealth and personal success. But among certain East Coast social circles, ancestry and appearances are as important as—if not more important than—personal achievement. A look at Jacqueline Lee Bouvier's maternal and paternal clans shows why not all prominent families are created equal. And those differing influences would have a profound influence on the young Jackie.

Family Lineage

Although she would one day be considered American royalty by many of her admirers, Jacqueline Lee Bouvier's family tree had decidedly common and middle-class roots. The Lee patriarch in America had fled nineteenth-century Ireland to escape starvation and disease. His hard-working descendants slowly climbed up the social ladder, never quite losing their scrappy blue-collar mentality. Considered *nouveau riche*, the Lees struggled to find acceptance among old-money New York aristocrats—such as the Bouviers, one of the few Catholic families included in New York's Protestant-heavy *Social Register*.

QUESTION

What was the *Social Register* and who was in it?

The original New York *Social Register* was a list of the city's most prominent and influential families. It was first compiled by Louis Keller in 1887. Being wealthy was only one criterion; families also had to be socially acceptable. As such, blacks, Jews, and Catholics were seldom included.

The Lees

James Thomas Lee was an overachiever. His grandparents, Thomas and Frances, had come to America from County Cork, Ireland, and went to work at a rubber company to support their six children. His father, James Lee, had been a teacher and his mother, Mary Norton, a nurse. James Thomas, called Jim, had much loftier goals.

Born in 1877, he received an engineering degree from New York's City College and earned a law degree three years later from Columbia University. Jim was a short, impatient man who kept fit by boxing for a half hour every day. He was also ambitious. He quit his job as a law clerk and opened his own practice.

In 1903 Jim married Margaret Merritt, described by acquaintances as a gentle woman whose parents were also Irish immigrants.

Jim and Margaret had three daughters: Marion, Janet, and Winifred. Jim gave up law and went into real estate. A shrewd and daring businessman, he became a multimillionaire by building and renting out luxury apartment buildings.

FACT

Overall, 1.8 million people left Ireland between 1846 and 1855. Out of the emigrants, nine-tenths of those migrated to the United States. Seventy-five percent of those immigrants settled in New York. By 1850, New York City had more Irish-born citizens than Dublin.

Being rich wasn't enough for Jim, though; he also wanted respect. Despite his position as chairman of New York Central Savings Bank and his wealth, which by 1922 was estimated to be in excess of $35 million, the Lees remained on the outer fringes of high society, lacking the right "pedigree."

The Bouviers

Not long after Napoleon was defeated at Waterloo in 1815, Michel Bouvier, a young cabinetmaker from Provence, arrived in Philadelphia and amassed a fortune as a talented cabinetmaker and designer. He used his money to buy more than 150,000 acres of land in coal-rich West Virginia as well as real estate in Philadelphia's posh Main Line neighborhood. After his first wife died, Michel married Louise Vernou.

Of Michel's nine children, only two survived to adulthood: Michel (called M. C.) and John Vernou. After their father died in 1874, the Bouvier brothers invested the family money in real estate and the stock market. By 1914, they had amassed a fortune equivalent to $40 million in today's dollars. They were readily accepted by New York's society elite and were listed in the *Social Register* despite their Catholic faith.

> **FACT**
> One of Michel's first customers was Napoleon Bonaparte's older brother, Joseph. After Napoleon's defeat at Waterloo, Joseph moved to the United States. He first settled in Philadelphia but later moved to an estate in New Jersey, which he named Point Breeze. Although he used the pseudonym Count de Survilliers, his neighbors called him Mr. Bonaparte.

The Major

John Vernou Bouvier married Caroline Ewing, one of New York's most beautiful socialites. Their son, John Vernou Jr., earned his law degree at Columbia and was a well-regarded trial attorney. In 1890 he married Maude Sergeant and they raised five children: John Vernou III, William Sergeant, Edith, and the twins Maude and Michelle. They grew up in a twenty-four-room apartment on Park Avenue. During the summer, the Bouviers relocated to their East Hampton estate, Lasata, where they stayed until the pumpkin harvest.

During World War I, John was appointed major judge advocate for the army by Supreme Court Justice Benjamin Cardozo. From then on, John Vernou Jr. preferred being addressed as "The Major." After the war ended, he gave up his private practice and went to work for his Uncle Michel's Wall Street firm.

Revisionist History

The Major was as dapper as James Thomas Lee was rough around the edges. Long after they were out of fashion, he continued to sport spats, starched collars, tweed jackets, and a waxed mustache—the very picture of upper-crust gentility. But the two men shared one common trait—the tendency to dabble in revisionist history.

Jim Lee would go to extraordinary lengths to secure his family's position—including fabricating his background. In a listing submitted to the *National Cyclopedia of American Biography*, which included short articles about historically important families, James completely denied his parents' heritage. Instead, he claimed his father had been born in Maryland and served as a Confederate soldier during the Civil War. Similarly, Margaret's father, Thomas Merritt, was identified as being a Savannah, Georgia, native who made his living as an importer and was also a Confederate veteran.

Just as Jim Lee erased his Irish heritage, John Vernou Jr. embellished his family tree. He wrote a book called *Our Forebears* in which he claimed the Bouviers were descended from French aristocrats with ties to the monarchy. None of it was true, but it reflected John Vernou Jr.'s sense of entitlement and elitism.

THEY SAID...

"No wonder, then, that his children and grandchildren assimilated an unfortunate kind of folie de grandeur, a sense that their progenitors were so eminent, their privileged place so much their due, that the Bouviers were a tribe apart. For lesser mortals even to meet them ought to be benediction enough in this life."

—Donald Spoto, *Jacqueline Bouvier Kennedy Onassis*

As desperately as Jim Lee wanted to be included in the world of high society, the Major wanted to ensure his family remained at the top of the pecking order. Their best-laid plans collided when Janet Norton Lee set her sights on John Vernou Bouvier III.

A Promising Romance

Despite their sixteen-year age difference, Janet and John Vernou seemed well matched emotionally. She was responsible to a fault and mature beyond her years; he was still Peter Pan, clinging to the carefree behavior of youth. Plus, the couple shared a mutual ambition: to be as rich as possible. Money didn't merely pay for a lavish lifestyle; it was the currency that kept them socially desirable. But the union of the clans would prove to be a disastrous marital mix of personalities that would ultimately give Jacqueline Bouvier a cynical view of men and a coolly practical regard for relationships.

The Southern Belle

Determined to marry into money and prestige, Janet carefully groomed herself for a life of sophistication. She studied French, learned to ride, and mastered the art of stroking men's egos. Petite and outgoing, Janet had plenty of potential suitors eager to spend time with her. She propagated James's fabrication of coming from the "Maryland Lees" so often and with such conviction that she began thinking of herself as a true Southern belle.

Among the friends she made in East Hampton were Maude and Michelle Bouvier, who regularly invited her to summer parties at Lasata. Janet was twenty when she caught the eye of their older brother, John Vernou Bouvier III, in 1927. With his Hollywood handsome looks, slicked-back hair, thin mustache, and dark complexion that gave him a sensual, exotic appearance, the Bouvier scion was known by everyone as Black Jack. And Janet was smitten.

FACT

Lasata was designed by architect Arthur Jackson and built in 1917. It sat on fourteen acres of land filled with fruit trees, an apple orchard, and a cornfield. In addition to the stables, paddock, and horse-jumping ring, there was also a tennis court, a fishpond, and sunken gardens. The name of the estate comes from the Shinnecock word meaning "place of peace."

Black Jack

A Yale graduate, Jack was a stockbroker by trade. But his primary pursuits were women, drinking, gambling, and living the high life. Despite earning millions in the 1920s, Jack spent money as quickly as he earned it and often had to borrow from his father or uncle to pay off his bills. Regardless of his reputation as a hard-living playboy, Black Jack was one of New York's most eligible bachelors, so he never lacked for female companionship. But the relationships were more diversions than serious attempts to settle down. Janet intended to change that.

The flirtation that began in East Hampton continued once Jack and Janet returned to Manhattan. Jack took Janet to fancy society parties and smoky speakeasies. They ate at five-star restaurants and went dancing afterward. Finally, at Easter in 1928, they announced their engagement. But even though Black Jack was getting married, Janet quickly discovered that didn't mean he intended to settle down.

Newlyweds

Janet and Jack were married in front of 500 guests on July 7, 1928, in East Hampton's St. Philomena Catholic Church. The Lees hosted the reception at their rented East Hampton home, Avery Place. After spending the night in New York at the Plaza Hotel, the newlyweds left for a honeymoon cruise to Europe. When they returned at the end of August, they moved into Jack's small apartment.

Despite being neighbors both in Manhattan and at the beach, neither family was overly enthused about the union—or each other. The Bouviers believed Janet was marrying Jack to better her social standing. And while Jack was generous and came from exactly the kind of family Jim Lee wanted his daughter married into, he was hardly dependable husband material.

Predictably, the honeymoon was short-lived. Jack quickly fell back into Manhattan's party scene and his drinking became excessive. He slept with other women, sometimes staying out all night. Janet tried to ignore his boorish behavior and filled her day with diversions—she shopped, she rode horses, she entertained. But when Jack drank himself to the point of a coma on New Year's Eve 1928, Janet's friends and family began to worry that the marriage might have been a mistake. By that time, however, Janet was pregnant. Black Jack was about to be a father.

A Double Catastrophe

Jacqueline Lee Bouvier was born July 28, 1929, on a stiflingly hot Sunday in Southampton. Janet wanted her daughter's name to be pronounced the French "Jaques-leen" but Jack called her Jackie.

Bud Bouvier

The joy of Jackie's birth was tempered in the autumn of 1929 by two equally traumatic events. On October 7, Jack's younger brother Bud died. He was just thirty-six. While the official cause of death was acute alcohol poisoning, some believed he was yet another casualty of the Great War. Bud had been attending Yale when World War I broke out. Angered over the German invasion of France, he dropped out his senior year to enlist in the army. He excelled and quickly rose through the ranks to captain. His division was sent to France, where he fought in several major confrontations and was gassed while participating in the Meuse-Argonne offensive. Bud was sent home to recuperate, but friends and family say he never fully recovered from the experience.

FACT

The Meuse-Argonne offensive was the largest and final operation of World War I. It was also one of the deadliest. During the six weeks of fighting, 26,277 American forces were killed and another 95,786 were wounded. The American victory over Germany's army led directly to the end of the war on November 11, 1918.

In the years after the war, Bud became an aimless drinker. The family intervened several times, sending him to rehabs in New Jersey, Connecticut, and even California. The lure of the bottle proved too great. His marriage ended in divorce, and Bud died drunk and alone in California. Bud left his son, Miche, in Jack's care, and the boy became an unofficial big brother to Jackie and her younger sister.

The Crash

Eight days after Bud's death, the stock market crashed. At first, it looked as if Black Jack might come out all right. Sensing trouble in the market, he had sold his shares short and earned $100,000. But the prices kept falling, and by November he had lost all the money. The Major suffered significant losses but maintained his lifestyle by living on savings while he waited for the real estate market to pick back up. The only one who remained financially secure was Jack's uncle, M. C. Bouvier. He had no debt and a hard cash reserve of $1.6 million. Including his various bonds, his total assets amounted to nearly $4 million.

For Black Jack, the future was financially bleak. By this point in his life, he had squandered millions of dollars on a reckless, self-indulgent lifestyle and had nothing to show for his years on Wall Street. The crash became a full-blown economic depression, and his source of income dried up to practically nothing.

He asked his family for help, but the only one in a position to help was M. C. Instead of the $1 million Jack wanted—the equivalent of over $11 million in today's dollars—M. C. gave him a $25,000 loan. Jack was insulted and angry.

Although it would take until the start of World War II for the country to fully recover from the Great Depression, Janet and Jack borrowed money, lived on credit, and went into debt to continue to live in the style to which they had become accustomed. Thanks to the generosity of his parents, who rented them a summer cottage, they continued to spend the seasons in East Hampton, a magical time that would have a lasting impact on Jackie.

The Bouvier Sisters

From the time she was born, Jackie was a daddy's girl, with a creamy complexion, thick brunette hair, and inquisitive brown eyes. When she was little, he lavished her with encouragement and praise. As she grew older, he expressed pride in her accomplishments. They shared confidences and a unique emotional bond. Even when Jackie became aware that her father was a womanizing, functional alcoholic, she accepted his failings unconditionally. Throughout her life she regarded him as a dashing, charismatic figure. She was clearly his favorite, which became an unspoken source of tension between Jackie and her sister. Caroline Lee Bouvier, four years younger than Jackie, went by her middle name in an effort to please her maternal grandfather.

> ## THEY SAID...
> "From the beginning it was a rivalry in which Lee, except for brief periods, was always the loser, Jackie the star. Lee felt this most strongly in their relationship with their father: Black Jack adored both his daughters and was proud of their looks and accomplishments, but his passion for Jackie (and hers for him) was overriding and semi-incestuous."
>
> —Sarah Bradford, *America's Queen*

Even as young children, Jackie and Lee had a complicated relationship. On one hand, they were as close as any two sisters, being playmates and companions. Lee looked up to Jackie, who in turn felt protective of her younger sibling. But their innate devotion to each other was tempered by an undercurrent of rivalry for the affection, attention, and pride of their parents, in particular Black Jack.

Although knowing Jackie was the favorite hurt Lee, there was little she could do about it. She lacked Jackie's riding skills and general athleticism. Being four years younger, Lee would always be overshadowed by the accomplishments of her vivacious big sister. It was a dynamic that would fester throughout their childhood and youth.

Summers in the Hamptons

The problems of the Great Depression seemed very far away from the white sands of East Hampton. The Bouviers kept up appearances as a happily married, prosperous society couple.

Family and Fun

Janet wasted no time teaching Jackie to ride, and by the age of two she was able to confidently control her pony. Her competitive and determined nature particularly showed itself when she was learning to ride—if she fell off, she would jump up and climb back on without a moment's hesitation.

The center of summer life was at Lasata. John and Maude threw lavish parties at the nearby Devon Yacht Club and spent Sundays surrounded by family for a traditional lunch of roast beef with homemade peach ice cream for dessert. Jackie called her grandfather Grampy Jack, and he doted on her. Of his ten grandchildren, she was the clear favorite, and he instilled in her his love of poetry and literature. He often recited poems he had written or read Shakespeare aloud to teach Jackie and the other children the importance of literature.

THEY SAID...

"She gave [Grampy Jack] great pleasure. It was mutual, and it was very nice to watch them together. I think that if it hadn't been for this exceptional bond she had with my grandfather Bouvier and my father that she never would have gained the particular strength and independence and individuality she had."

—Lee Radziwill, in *America's Queen*

During the week, Jackie spent most of her time with animals—her horse, Danseuse, and her Scottish terrier, Hootchie. She participated in equestrian events and entered Hootchie in the East Hampton dog show. As she got older, she'd spend more time with her cousins Scotty, Miche, and John Davis. But her most eccentric relative was Black Jack's sister, Edie.

Big Edie

While other women of her era longed for the security of a good marriage, Edith Ewing Bouvier wanted to be a performer. The Major wouldn't hear of it, and he pushed her into an unwanted marriage. The marriage didn't last, and Edie moved into Grey Gardens, a large house near East Hampton's Georgia Beach. Big Edie lived in the extravagantly uncared for house with her stunningly beautiful daughter, Little Edie, who was considered the family beauty.

SHE SAID...

"I hated dolls and loved horses and dogs. . . . I read a lot when I was little, much of which was too old for me. There were Chekhov and Shaw in the room where I had to take naps and I never slept but sat on the windowsill reading. . . . My heroes were Byron, Mowgli, Robin Hood, Little Lord Fauntleroy's grandfather, and Scarlett O'Hara."

Big Edie's was one of Jackie's favorite hideouts because her aunt was not big on social graces. Hers was a relaxed, informal home. She entertained Jackie by playing the piano and singing songs, from Gershwin to opera. Independent, unaffected, and just a little wacky, she was considered by the other adults to be a bad influence—which of course made her that much more popular with her nieces and nephews.

For as long as Jackie could remember, East Hampton had been her special place. It was the foundation of her closeness to the Bouvier side of her family, especially her grandfather. But as Janet and Jack's marriage slowly fell apart, the good times at the beach came to an end.

A Bitter End

The steady disintegration of Jack and Janet's marriage had a profound effect on their children. Black Jack's affairs were a source of constant humiliation for Janet, who frequently took out her frustrations on Jackie and Lee. She was constantly critical of them and frequently lashed out physically. Several relatives witnessed her slapping Jackie in an irrational rage. Hot-headed in the best of times, Janet was pushed to the limit by her husband and felt betrayed by her children. She was sharply aware that the girls favored their father over her. Janet particularly resented Jackie's emotional distance and her continued adoration of Black Jack when it was his womanizing that was destroying the marriage. Even so, he could do no wrong in Jackie's eyes.

Living Large

Money remained a huge issue. Jack continued to live beyond his means, so he was chronically in debt. Janet was angry that there wasn't enough money for a larger staff to help her run the apartment. Jim Lee used Jack's misfortune to try to rein his son-in-law in. In 1932, Jim let Jack and Janet move into his apartment building at 740 Park Avenue, a gorgeous eleven-room duplex, and live there rent-free. In exchange, he expected Jack to cut his expenses and be more responsible. Jack was deeply resentful that Janet's father would interfere in his marriage and personal life, and it deepened the rift between them.

After M. C.'s death in 1935, Jack inherited his uncle's clients. He opened a brokerage company and over the following year earned $35,000—but racked up more than $40,000 in expenses. M. C.'s estate pressured Jack to repay the $25,000 loan he had borrowed in 1930, and he was deeply in arrears with the IRS.

Acting Out

The family was slowly imploding, and Jack and Janet's constant arguing had a deep effect on Jackie. Outwardly, she was angry at their constant arguing, but inwardly she was afraid to lose her family and felt helpless to stop it. Jackie started acting out, throwing temper tantrums when she was angry or couldn't get her way.

One family maid recalled the time Black Jack would not allow Jackie to go to a movie with several of her ten-year-old friends unless an adult went with them. She threw such a tantrum Jack eventually gave in. Her temper would explode over the smallest incidents, from having to wait to use the tennis court to not having a towel waiting for her when she finished swimming. But her usual way of dealing with the slow disintegration of her parents' marriage and their mutual bitterness was to tune them out and escape into literature and horse riding.

Separation

In September 1936, Janet finally asked for a trial separation. Jack moved into a nearby hotel while she continued living at the

SHE SAID...

"When I go down to the sandy shore,

I can think of nothing I want more

Than to live by the booming blue sea,

As the seagulls flutter around about me

I can run about when the tide is out,

With the wind and the sea all about

And the seagulls are swirling and div-

ing for fish, Oh—to live by the sea is

my only wish."—"Sea Joy,"

a poem by Jacqueline Bouvier,

written in 1939

apartment with their daughters. They reconciled the following summer but it would be the family's last summer in East Hampton together. When they returned to New York, they separated again, this time for good.

For the 1938 season, Janet rented a house forty miles outside of East Hampton, wanting to keep as much distance from Jack—and the gossiping neighbors—as possible. Jackie and Lee spent August with their father at Lasata, but it was no longer the happy home it used to be. Not only was Jack and Janet's marriage ending, but also the Major and Maude were going through their own drama. They had been quietly living separately for years, but that summer, Maude found out that Grampy Jack had fallen in love with another woman. When Maude died less than two years later, Big Edie claimed it was from a broken heart.

Divorce

On January 26, 1940, the *New York Daily Mirror* ran an article titled, "Society Broker Sued for Divorce." Included were details of Jack's infidelities, including pictures of his mistresses and even dates of their rendezvous. Newspapers across the country picked up the story, publicly trumpeting the private details of a destroyed marriage. It's believed Janet's lawyer had leaked the information to embarrass Jack. It also humiliated Jackie and instilled a dislike for and distrust of the media that would last a lifetime. Deeply pained by the barbs, insults, and accusations her parents hurled at one another, she became reserved and withdrawn at school—which was often mistaken for aloofness.

Jack, who did not want a divorce, turned the tables and accused Janet of being an unfit, abusive mother. Fearing loss of custody, she dropped the divorce. Janet took her daughters to Nevada and stayed six weeks—long enough to establish residency. In July 1940, she went to a Nevada court and filed for divorce there, claiming irreconcilable differences. The judge granted the divorce. Black Jack was officially no longer a part of Jackie's daily life. The resentment the young girl felt toward her mother would never completely go away.

A New Stepfather

Janet had fought hard to get her independence from Jack. Now she faced the daunting prospect of supporting her daughters—and her desired lifestyle—as a divorced mother of two young girls. Her father made her move out of the Park Avenue apartment into a more modest building he owned. She worked as a model for Macy's and took courses to be a nurse's aide. But her primary objective was to find a new husband who could both lavishly support her and make her once again acceptable to high society.

While she was in Nevada waiting to divorce Jack, Janet met Esther Auchincloss Nash. Esther was the granddaughter of one of the original founding partners of Standard Oil. The two women commiserated about their womanizing husbands and became friends. Less than two years later, they would become sisters-in-law.

Hughdie

Hugh Dudley Auchincloss Jr. was the opposite of Black Jack. Hughdie was an average-looking, hard-working, serious-minded man. He started his professional life working in the U.S. government, first in the Commerce Department, then at the State Department. He left government service to found the investment firm Auchincloss, Parker and Redpath, which he started with a million-dollar loan from his oil heiress mother.

In 1941, Hughdie was on the verge of his second divorce. His first wife, an exotic Russian beauty named Maya de Chrapovitsky, had been gravely injured when she stepped too close to an airplane propeller. She recovered from the gruesome head wounds, but her personality remained forever altered. The couple divorced, and Hughdie got custody of their son Hugh Dudley III, called Yusha. Hughdie's next marriage was to Nina Gore Vidal. Together they had two children, Nina and Thomas. Hughdie separated from Nina in 1941 after he discovered she was having an affair with an admiral.

FACT

Nina's first husband was Eugene L. Vidal, who headed what today is the Federal Aviation Administration, or FAA. Their son is the famously outspoken author and playwright Gore Vidal. Gore's maternal grandfather, Thomas P. Gore, was a U.S. senator from Oklahoma; through that side of the family, Vidal is distantly related to former vice president Al Gore.

Courtship

Depressed about her circumstances, angry she had to "scrape by" on Jack's monthly $1,100 alimony payments—the equivalent of around $15,000 today—Janet sought to cheer herself up by taking a trip to the Caribbean in 1941 with a group of friends. While there, she met Hughdie, who was there with his own group of pals. Janet let him know she was a friend of Esther's and proceeded to sweep Hughdie off his feet.

Janet's friends found Hughdie dull—his stepson Gore called him a "magnum of chloroform"—but he was everything Janet wanted. He was dependable and gentlemanly, and his family was staggeringly rich. Forty-seven Auchinclosses were listed in the 1941 *Social Register.* Back in New York, Hughdie and Janet began dating very quietly. Not taking anything for granted, Janet also continued dating other men as well. She needn't have worried. Hughdie was thoroughly smitten and asked her to marry him.

Janet Norton Lee Bouvier Auchincloss

Hughdie and Janet were married on June 21, 1942, in Washington, D.C. Jackie and Lee did not attend the ceremony because the marriage was arranged so quickly and because of wartime travel restrictions. They were staying with their maternal grandparents when their mother called to inform them. Lee later commented that their first question was which man she had married, since at the time Janet had more than one suitor. Two days later, Hughdie shipped out to work with British intelligence in Jamaica. After traveling to Connecticut to meet her new mother-in-law, who was too ill to go to Washington for the ceremony, Janet went to stay with her daughters at the Lees' East Hampton house.

Once Hughdie returned, all their children—Jackie, Lee, Yusha, Nina, and Tommy—were brought to Hughdie's Merrywood estate in McLean, Virginia, outside the nation's capital, for their wedding reception. Merrywood became Jackie's primary residence for the rest of her teen years. Yusha, who had a harmless crush on his new stepsister, became Jackie's closest stepsibling and one of her most trusted confidants.

Chapter 2

NEW YORK CAFÉ SOCIETY

For most of the country, the lean years of the Great Depression were fraught with uncertainty and hardship. But for Manhattan's wealthiest citizens, life in the 1930s and early 1940s went on as usual. They spent summers at the beach in Long Island and consumed conspicuously when back in the city. Dubbed the café society, they ate at the right restaurants, lived in the right buildings, and partied at the right nightclubs. The richest got richer and everyone else in the social elite tried to keep up.

Keeping Up with the Blue-Blooded Joneses

In America, the color of royalty is green—as in hard, cold cash. But longevity and breeding counted too, insomuch as they determined whether a family was considered nouveau riche gauche or well-bred old money. Among the East Coast's upper social echelon, a select few families stood head and shoulders above the others. And nothing reflected status quite as much as the family home.

Many descendants of the Gilded Age millionaires and billionaires lived in almost obscene splendor. For example, railroad tycoon Cornelius Vanderbilt II's summer house in Newport, The Breakers, was completed in 1895 and cost $7 million to build—a price tag that would be in excess of $200 million today. It had seventy rooms, including thirty-three for household help—and it was empty for ten months out of the year.

FACT

Despite the extravagance of The Breakers, Cornelius Vanderbilt II was considered a generous philanthropist and gave away large chunks of the $70 million inheritance he received from his father. His granddaughter is fashion designer Gloria Vanderbilt, and his great-grandson is CNN news anchor Anderson Cooper.

Back in the city, by the early twentieth century, the Upper East Side became a *Social Register* stronghold. Charmed by scenic views of Central Park's lush greenery and the area's central location, New York's wealthiest flocked to the area, building stately town homes.

Fifth Avenue

In the early twentieth century, upper Fifth Avenue was considered the Gold Coast of Manhattan. With its views of Central Park and proximity to museums and the best clubs and restaurants, it was a haven for the rich and famous.

THEY SAID...

"It is quite probable that the world had never seen nor will ever see again such a concentration of wealth as that represented by the mansions that were built on upper Fifth Avenue from 1890 until World War I. Millionaires' residences stretched for a solid mile and a half from Fifty-ninth Street to Ninetieth."

—James Theodore Jr., *Fifth Avenue*

Prior to World War I, nearly 90 percent of private residences along Fifth Avenue were single-family mansions or townhouses. By 1940, 90 percent lived in multiunit apartment buildings. The change was attributed to changing zoning laws, an increased population, and skyrocketing property taxes.

After World War I, it became fashionable to sell the family mansion and move into the sumptuous apartments that were springing up all over Upper Manhattan. The first notable building was at 998 Fifth Avenue at Eighty-first Street, designed to resemble Italian palazzos. Most of the buildings that sprang up all along Fifth and Park Avenues in the 1920s and 1930s were only eleven or twelve stories tall. An individual apartment usually covered an entire floor—sometimes two—and offered all the luxuries of homeownership without the expensive upkeep.

THEY SAID...

"The Bouviers accustomed Jackie to elegant living. . . . 'Jackie,' her father once told her, 'you never have to worry about keeping up with the Joneses, because we are the Joneses. Everybody has to keep up with us.'"

—Paul F. Boller, *Presidential Wives*

While few of the buildings could match the grandeur of the 998 Fifth Avenue building, the apartments were known for their spacious rooms and breathtaking views, and the residences quickly gained popularity. When Jackie's grandfather James Lee built his Park Avenue building and charged $2,000 per month for rent for each unit, many thought he was crazy. Instead, he made millions.

Playgrounds of the Rich and Famous

Having wealth has always meant having the freedom to live lavishly, travel extensively, and indulge in expensive entertainments. Jackie grew up acutely aware that an abundance of money was necessary to maintain such a lifestyle and to guarantee the creature comforts she had become accustomed to. In her world, money meant independence and exclusivity. It also meant enjoying the good life.

The Hamptons

An area originally settled by Puritans, the Hamptons refers collectively to the towns and hamlets dotting the southern tip of Long Island. In the late nineteenth century the village of East Hampton became an enclave for artists and a summer playground for many of the East Coast's old-money families, such as the Du Ponts and the Mellons, who were drawn by the area's immaculate white sand beaches and rustic woods.

> **FACT**
>
> East Hampton attracted its share of eccentric residents, such as the wife of artist Albert Herter, known for completely replanting her garden overnight so that guests would enjoy different flower presentations every day.

Newport, Rhode Island

Newport's mild summer weather made it a popular vacation destination long before the rich discovered it. But when Mrs. William Astor, one of New York's most influential socialites, began retreating to Newport for the summer season, it became an important social gathering spot. The Astors purchased their Newport estate, Beechwood, in 1881, and hired noted architect Richard Morris Hunt to supervise a $2 million renovation.

Beechwood became the center of Newport social life during the eight-week summer season. Mrs. Astor hosted a summer ball and threw exclusive dinner parties. The privileged few who were invited were attended by a brigade of servants. Mrs. Astor was the doyenne of New York and Newport society for more than two decades. She died at Beechwood in 1908, and the estate is now a living-history museum.

SHE SAID . . .

"I'll never forget the night my mother and father both came into my bedroom all dressed up to go out. I can still smell the scent my mother wore and feel the softness of her fur coat as she leaned over to kiss me goodnight. . . . It was one of the few times I remember seeing my parents together. It was so romantic. So hopeful."

By the time Janet married Hughdie, more than 100 estate homes had been built to join Beechwood. Although Jackie would visit her father at Lasata, she spent most of her teen summers at Hammersmith Farm, the Auchincloss's Newport estate.

Speakeasies

During Prohibition, thousands of illegal bars called speakeasies sprang up throughout New York. Some were little more than isolated shacks where the poor and middle class risked their lives drinking homemade swill. Other speakeasies were glamorous, popular nightclubs that attracted a clientele wealthy enough to afford the champagne and liquor smuggled into the country by organized crime. Among the most famous speakeasies were Jack and Charlie's 21 Club on Fifty-second Street and the Cotton Club up in Harlem.

FACT
Speakeasies got their name from the need of patrons to whisper or speak easy when giving the secret password necessary for admittance. In the nicer establishments, owners would provide entertainment for the customers to enjoy while they drank.

Private Clubs

Not only were private clubs a place for men to get away from children, wives, girlfriends, and mistresses, they were also important status symbols. Some were strictly social, like the Metropolitan, located at the corner of Sixtieth and Fifth Avenue. Commissioned by J. P. Morgan and designed by Stanford White, the Metropolitan had 700 members, including Whitneys, Vanderbilts, and Roosevelts.

Other private clubs were both fitness clubs and sanctuaries. The Downtown Athletic Club offered stressed lawyers and businessmen a wide variety of activities, including a swimming pool, squash and tennis courts, and a miniature golf course. Members could eat dinner on the premises and get a room for an overnight stay. The Athletic Club was best known to the rest of America as the home of the Heisman Trophy, awarded annually to the most outstanding college football player.

FACT

Stanford White was one of America's most prolific, influential, and respected architects. He designed many of New York's more famous buildings, including the original Madison Square Garden, but his private life was scandalous. Known as a womanizer, he had a weakness for seducing teenage girls. White was murdered in 1906 by the jealous husband of one of his former lovers.

Central Park

Central Park was the first landscaped public park in America. Although Manhattan's wealthiest laid claim to the park by building luxurious homes along its eastern border, New Yorkers from all walks of life flocked to it. But its history reflects the ongoing class struggle that was as much a part of New York life as the steamy humidity of summer and the brittle chill of winter.

> ## THEY SAID...
>
> "Advocates of creating the park—primarily wealthy merchants and landowners—admired the public grounds of London and Paris and urged that New York needed a comparable facility to establish its international reputation. A public park . . . would offer their own families an attractive setting for carriage rides and provide working-class New Yorkers with a healthy alternative to the saloon."
>
> —Elizabeth Blackmar and Roy Rosenzweig,
> *The Park and the People*

One of the first obstacles in building the park was deciding who should control a public park. Initially, state politicians appointed the Central Park commissioner. Later, the city balked and passed a charter that gave the mayor control over park appointments. Politics was only one issue; where to locate the park was debated by business owners and residents who were anxious to improve the value of their neighborhoods, as long as it didn't infringe on their lifestyle.

The city eventually chose to purchase more than 800 acres of swampy, rocky land between Fifth and Eighth Avenues and 59th and 110th Streets. A contest was held and in 1857 the Central Park Commission selected a design submitted by Calvert Vaux and Frederick Law Olmsted. It took more than 20,000 workers to smoothe, reshape, and landscape the original topography into a breathtaking urban sanctuary. Lakes, bridges, sprawling meadows, dense woods, scenic paths, and 270,000 newly planted trees created a magical escape from the noise, bustle, and dirt of city life.

After it opened in 1859, the park became a popular place for wealthy socialites to go for carriage rides in the late afternoon. By the 1930s, the richest New Yorkers lived all along the eastern side of the park, using it as if it were their personal front yard. Jackie would often go for strolls in the park with her father, who would borrow dogs from local pet stores to accompany them. It was the beginning of Jackie's life-long love affair with Central Park.

FACT

Central Park covers 6 percent of Manhattan. After the state legislature approved the city's use of eminent domain in 1853 to purchase land for the park, more than 1,600 of New York's poorest were left homeless. Among those displaced were Irish pig farmers, New York's first important settlement of African Americans, and an assortment of German gardeners.

The Met

The Metropolitan Museum of Art opened on February 20, 1872, in a building located at 681 Fifth Avenue. Its first president was railroad executive John Taylor Johnston, whose personal art collection was a large part of the museum's initial holdings that included 174 paintings and a Roman stone sarcophagus. Publisher George Palmer Putnam was its founding superintendent.

After outgrowing its location, the Met temporarily moved to West Fourteenth Street. In 1880, the city of New York agreed to let the museum relocate to Central Park along upper Fifth Avenue, which became its permanent home. Calvert Vaux, who had also designed the park, designed the original building. Over the following fifty years, many wings and façades were added.

Eastside, Westside, All Around the Town

The width of Central Park may be only three city blocks long, but the gulf between the Upper West Side and the Upper East Side first widened as soon as the two disparate neighborhoods became populated in the years following the opening of the park.

Upper West Side

The Upper West Side, which is anything west of Central Park and north of Fifty-ninth Street, has always attracted more bohemian residents. Intellectuals, artists, and others in creative fields settled there in increasing numbers after World War I.

By the turn of the century, many Russian Jewish immigrants, who originally settled on the Lower East Side, began looking for living quarters uptown as their businesses prospered. But new money in general—and Jews in particular—were not made welcome on the Upper East Side. Seeing an opportunity, some of the earliest apartment buildings on the Upper West Side were built by developers specifically looking to attract Jewish tenants.

Upper East Side

Up until construction began on the Metropolitan Museum, the Upper East Side was mostly pastureland. But the cachet of the museum prompted some big money names to buy land nearby to build houses. Stanford White designed a house for Charles Tiffany a block east of the Park. But the person who "made" the Upper East Side was society maven Caroline Astor who commissioned a château to be built at Sixty-fifth and Fifth.

Over the next decade, dozens of high society families built homes along Fifth Avenue, earning it the nickname Millionaire's Row. Not long after, private clubs such as the Metropolitan and the Knickerbocker opened in the area to accommodate the local residents. Once the train tracks were removed and the street paved, Fourth Avenue was renamed Park Avenue. Along with Fifth and Madison Avenues, these streets east of the park became New York's most sought after addresses by the status conscious.

The East Siders were very class conscious and regarded artists and intellectuals as inferior, albeit occasionally fascinating. They viewed the nouveau riche with tacit disdain. Although Upper East Side residents considered themselves the social trendsetters in the pre-World War II era, they eventually took a cue from the West Side. By the early 1940s, most of the extravagant single-family manses along Fifth Avenue gave way to million-dollar apartments.

Society Hotspots

The divide between rich and poor never seemed more noticeable as during the Depression years. While the majority of New Yorkers struggled to earn enough to buy decent food, the city's elite enjoyed fine restaurants, music clubs, and nights out on the town. Up in Harlem, the Cotton Club was just one of dozens of hotspots favored by high society.

To See and Be Seen

Like other clubs of the era, the Stork Club began as a speakeasy. Known for its famous—and infamous—clientele, which ranged from actors and politicians to sports figures and mobsters, the Stork Club laid the foundation for modern celebrity. Owned by an ex-con named Sherman Billingsley, the Stork Club had a VIP section that catered to gossip columnists like Walter Winchell in order to keep the club's name in society columns.

Opened in 1931, the El Morocco was as famous for its blue zebra décor as it was its clientele. The owner was an Italian immigrant named John Perona, who originally opened the El Morocco as a speakeasy on East Fifty-fourth. The café society set flocked to the club in part because of in-house photographer Jerome Zerbe. He would take photos of the club's patrons and make sure they were printed in the next day's society columns.

Not far off Fifth Avenue was the Central Park Casino, which was owned by the city of New York. Casino, in this case, was the literal Italian translation, little house. With a black glass ballroom, a tulip pavilion, and seating for 600, it was considered one of the most elegant restaurants and fashionable nightclubs in Manhattan. Pianist and bandleader Eddie Duchin started his career at the Casino.

The Waldorf-Astoria

In the 1930s and '40s, the Waldorf-Astoria on Park Avenue was one of the most popular venues for high society functions. The original Waldorf, on Thirty-fourth St., had been torn down to make way for the Empire State Building. The relocated hotel spanned an entire city block and housed both hotel rooms and private apartments in the Waldorf Towers. Modern-day room service was said to have been introduced at the Waldorf.

The Starlight Roof was almost 200 feet long and had floor to ceiling windows overlooking Park Avenue and an outdoor balcony. Its most unique feature was a retractable roof. Big band leaders Glenn Miller and other top talent of the day performed at the Starlight, performances which were broadcast on radio. For several decades Guy Lombardo and his Royal Canadians performed at the Starlight Roof on New Year's Eve; it was a New York tradition.

The Industrial Barons

The richest of the old-money families of the Upper East Side had made the bulk of their fortunes during the industrial boom that began in the middle of the nineteenth century. Typically of Anglo-Saxon descent, many could trace their ancestry back to colonial times. Socially clannish, snobbish, and elitist, the ultrawealthy were also responsible for financing many of Manhattan's cultural landmarks, such as Rockefeller Center, Carnegie Hall, and Grand Central Terminal.

The Astors

The Astors built their billion-dollar fortune from the fur trade and real estate. The family patriarch, John Jacob Astor, was America's first recorded millionaire. His son, William Backhouse Astor, married Caroline Schermerhorn, and she reigned over New York high society for decades. In fact, she was the one who literally defined it as "The 400." This was said to be the number of guests Mrs. Astor's ballroom could accommodate.

Although Caroline died in 1908, New York's high society remained, and the Astor family continued among them. Her nephew, William Vincent Astor, inherited $200 million in 1912 when his father, John Jacob Astor IV, died on the *Titanic*. Throughout the 1930s and 1940s, Vincent became known as a great philanthropist and was the chairman of *Newsweek* magazine, one of the Astor family holdings.

FACT

During the Kennedy administration, the United States assisted Egypt in removing historic structures that were threatened by the building of the Aswan Dam. Egypt expressed its gratitude by presenting the United States with one of the structures, the Temple of Dendur. Jacqueline Kennedy was instrumental in selecting the temple, which is now housed in the Metropolitan Museum of Art.

The Rockefellers

John D. Rockefeller revolutionized the oil industry. Through the Standard Oil Company, he became the world's first billionaire. But he also believed that great wealth demanded great philanthropy. He established foundations that were devoted to specific causes that included medical research and education. Over his lifetime, he donated more than $500 million to his pet causes. During the Depression, he personally financed the construction of a fourteen-building complex in the middle of Manhattan. Through the Rockefeller Center, John became one of New York's largest real estate moguls.

Although John never drank, he wrote a letter that was published on the front page of the *New York Times* urging the repeal of Prohibition. He argued that the banning of alcohol simply increased disrespect for law.

QUESTION

What was Prohibition?

Prohibition refers to the years 1920–1933 when the Eighteenth Amendment to the Constitution made it illegal to manufacture, sell, or consume alcoholic beverages in the United States. Ironically, drinking in America increased dramatically during Prohibition and organized crime flourished. Prior to 1920, New York had 15,000 licensed bars. By 1928, there were more than 32,000 illegal speakeasies.

The Whitneys

William Collins Whitney was a financier and prominent attorney. He married Flora Payne, the daughter of a wealthy Cleveland businessman and sister of his college friend, Colonel Oliver Payne, who introduced them. Both William and Flora could trace their family tree back to the *Mayflower*.

The marriage produced five children. Their middle child, William Payne Whitney—who later changed his name to Payne Whitney—increased the family fortune with his investments in banking, real estate, oil, and railroads. He was also a generous philanthropist, donating $12 million to the New York Public Library. When he died in 1927, his estate was the largest ever probated up to that time in American history. His only son, John Hay "Jock" Whitney, was a very visible member of high society in the 1930s and 1940s. Charming and affable, he was also an astute businessman. He founded the country's first venture capital firm, J.H. Whitney & Co.

The Vanderbilts

William H. Vanderbilt was considered the richest man in the world. He had inherited $100 million from his father, Cornelius Vanderbilt, and within a decade had doubled the fortune through railroad investments. When he died his son, Frederick William, assumed that title. The Vanderbilts took wealth to a level never before seen in American society. Ironically, despite the family's vast wealth, they were initially regarded as high-society outcasts, considered crass and uncouth.

After William died in 1855, his sons William K. and Cornelius II took over the family empire and brought the family respectability. The Vanderbilts' inclusion in café society was complete when Cornelius's daughter Gertrude, who founded the Whitney Museum, married Harry Payne Whitney.

The Vanderbilts enjoyed their leisure pursuits and shamelessly spent money living the good life. All of William Henry's children lived in palatial Fifth Avenue mansions and owned summer cottages out of the city. Yachting, car racing, and horses were favorite family passions. But the Vanderbilt heirs also believed in giving back to society and became influential patrons of the arts and respected philanthropists.

Prominent Families

Both the Auchinclosses and Bouviers were among the first included on the New York *Social Register,* along with other prominent families such as the Astors and the Roosevelts. But even among the social elite there were levels of privilege. Old money WASPs were at the top of the pecking order. The Bouviers, on the other hand, were included in spite of being Catholic, a fact that colored their peers' perception of them.

Despite their wealth, the Lee's were hopelessly *nouveau* and classless in the eyes of the New York society matrons in charge of the all important invitation lists to the right dinners and parties. When Janet married Black Jack, his family name gave her new credibility. Her marriage to Hughdie furthered her inclusion—as did being the president's mother-in-law.

Chapter 3

GROWING UP INGÉNUE

While Jackie's relationship with her father was arguably the most important emotional cornerstone of her childhood, her mother's passion for money and social standing equally informed Jackie's personality—and priorities—as she grew from a young girl into a debutante.

Horse Sense

Equestrian show riding requires grit, determination, and passion. For anyone to corral these qualities is an achievement. For a child barely of kindergarten age, it is nothing short of remarkable. From the time Janet first set her in a saddle as a toddler, Jackie showed an innate understanding of horses and displayed her deeply competitive nature. But riding was more than a sport. It became an escape from the misery of constantly fighting parents. As an adult, Jackie used riding as a way to be alone with her thoughts and moods.

Competition

Under her mother's careful and methodical tutelage, Jackie learned the art of show riding. She began competing when she was five, taking third place with Janet in the family event at the East Hampton Horse Show. In 1937, she won the children-under-nine division at the Southampton Horse Show. A year later Jackie earned a blue ribbon at the East Hampton Horse Show and the following summer won her class at the 1939 Southampton. Jackie's skill filled her father with pride, and riding became one of their shared passions.

FACT

In May 1965, Jackie competed with her mother and her eight-year-old daughter, Caroline, in the family class at the annual St. Bernard's School Horse Show. The trio took second place. It was the only time the three would ever compete together and the last time Jackie rode with Janet at an equestrian event.

After the separation from Jack Bouvier, Janet had less time to devote to riding, although Jackie continued to compete. She won four blue ribbons at the 1941 East Hampton Show, and her horse,

Danseuse, was singled out for the number of championships she had won with both Janet and Jackie. Jackie also participated in the 1940 and 1941 National Horse Shows held in November at Madison Square Garden. In 1944, she emerged as the undisputed teenage equestrian on Long Island, winning shows at Southampton, East Hampton, Bridgehampton, and Smithtown.

After Janet married Hughdie, Jackie's interest in competitive riding cooled and as a result, Jackie eventually dropped out of the show circuit. But riding remained a significant part of her life. At Merrywood, she rode nearby trails and also participated in some local foxhunts.

Janet and Jackie pose with their horse, Stepaside, at the East Hampton Horse Show in 1937

Photo Credit: Morgan Collection/Hulton Archive/Getty Images

Jackie with Danseuse at the Vassar Horse Show in 1939

Photo Credit: Morgan Collection/Hulton Archive/Getty Images

Danseuse

While she was married to Black Jack, Janet had four horses that were stabled at Lasata. Jackie's favorite horse was the chestnut mare whose name meant "female dancer." Jackie called her Donny. Jackie won most of her competitions on Danseuse and became deeply attached to the mare. When she left to attend a three-year college prep boarding school in Connecticut, the Major agreed to have Danseuse boarded at the local stable. Jackie would go for long rides on Donny through the countryside, and in the winter, the mare would pull Jackie and her school friends in a sleigh through the snow.

Donny was with the family for more than twenty years, and when she died Jackie wrote an emotional tribute to the mare, calling her a lady who knew how lovely she was.

THEY SAID...

"They were so close and then this horse, Danseuse, was the trio in their relationship for a good ten years. My father, the horse and Jackie. I have a book . . . with nearly every letter he'd written to each of us—at least half of it was about this horse and the next step of what hunt team she could go into, what class she thought she could do next year at the Garden."

—Lee Radziwill, in *America's Queen*

Early Creative Flair

Jackie's athleticism was balanced by an artistic, creative side. Drawn to poetry and literature, she learned to read at a young age, and by the age of five she could recite memorized passages from *The Wonderful Wizard of Oz* and *Little Lord Fauntleroy*. Although Jackie frequently closed off emotionally and refrained from talking about her deepest feelings concerning her parents' difficult relationship and, later, divorce, she found release by expressing herself through writing verses and stories. Her first poems and stories were for her family, but as she got older she wrote for friends and classmates. She often illustrated her writing with hand-drawn pictures. As a teenager in boarding school she wrote articles for the school newspaper, *Salmagundy*. The paper also published cartoons she submitted about a character called Frenzied Frieda whose exploits regularly got her in trouble—not unlike Jackie, who still managed to rankle teachers with her mischievousness.

Her ability to draw led Jackie to start painting. She would create canvases for Christmas gifts and once wryly noted that they were decent enough that her mother would leave them up for a full month after the holidays were over before stashing them in a closet. Grampy Jack exposed Jackie to art as a young child, and as she got older she formally studied art history and was well versed in classic styles and artists.

One of Jackie's deepest passions was for live performance, be it music or dance. She was particularly enchanted by ballet. She took lessons as a little girl and quickly realized she only had average talent. But she never lost interest and eagerly devoured any book on the subject.

Jackie also enjoyed theater and in high school wrote a musical that was produced by the drama club. She admitted to her stepbrother Yusha Auchincloss that she would have loved to have been an actress but acknowledged she would never be willing to be a struggling, starving artist. She showed glimpses of her potential as a talented mimic, however, and entertained her classmates with impressions of teachers. Her natural ear also made learning new languages easy for Jackie. Janet had made sure that her daughters learned to speak French by insisting it be the only language allowed at the dinner table. Later, Jackie also became fluent in Spanish and Italian.

Life on the Country Estates

Janet's marriage meant leaving New York. Jackie and Lee moved with their mother to Hughdie's McLean, Virginia, winter home, Merrywood. Summers were spent at Hammersmith Farm, located just outside Newport, Rhode Island. The move was traumatic for Black Jack, who was no longer able to spend weekends with his daughters. Lee especially had a hard time adjusting to her new life, although Jackie adapted with relatively little angst, mostly because she fell in love with Merrywood, a lushly wooded fifty-acre estate near the bank of the Potomac River.

Merrywood

Hughdie bought Merrywood in 1934 for $135,000. He spent another $100,000 on additions, such as an indoor badminton court and a greenhouse to go along with the estate's existing luxuries: tennis courts, stables, an Olympic-size swimming pool, a huge library, and miles of riding trails. The Georgian-style home was extravagantly spacious. While the décor was a bit stuffy, with

Victorian furniture and stuffed animal heads adorning the walls, Jackie reveled in having her own bedroom.

FACT

The Potomac River basin was first settled 10,000 years ago by indigenous tribes, who were drawn by the river's plentiful supply of fish and crabs. The river begins in West Virginia and flows more than 380 miles through Appalachia to Chesapeake Bay at Point Lookout, Maryland. Because of its proximity to Washington, D.C., it's known as the Nation's River.

Jackie inherited Gore Vidal's old bedroom. It was painted a pale yellow and had a hand-painted flower mural on one wall. The room was decorated with white cane furniture. Through the window she could hear the gentle rush of the nearby Potomac. The bedroom became a sanctuary where she would go whenever she needed solitude to write, read, paint, or just be alone with her thoughts.

Hammersmith Farm

Perched on a hill overlooking Narragansett Bay in Newport, Rhode Island, the ninety-acre Hammersmith Farm was the size of a small village. The main house was built in 1887 for Hughdie's great-grandfather, John W. Auchincloss. It had twenty-eight rooms, including ten bedrooms and twelve bathrooms. A dozen fireplaces were scattered throughout.

The estate's sprawling rose and rock garden, spanning seventy-eight acres, was designed by Frederick Olmsted and Calvert Vaux, the same team who designed Central Park. There were five hothouses to grow and tend the plants. The grounds also housed stables, a carriage house, and an animal cemetery. Hammersmith's guesthouse was called the Windmill. Years later, Jackie would hold her wedding reception there.

Normally Auchincloss had a small army of employees to keep the house and tend to the land. During World War II, the staff was greatly reduced, as many had enlisted or gone to work at industrial manufacturers. Janet and her daughters were forced to pitch in. Jackie learned to cook and helped clean house. She also acted as Hammersmith's receptionist, answering the telephone and taking messages. Unable to care for the huge garden herself, Janet made the decision to reduce its size. Once it was more manageable, she put Jackie and Lee to work weeding and watering, a chore they ended up enjoying. Most of all, they took pride in the belief they were helping America's war effort.

Jackie on her tenth birthday with her dog Tammy

Photo Credit: Morgan Collection/Hulton Archive/Getty Images

Hammersmith was a functional farm. In fact, it was the oldest—and last—working farm in Newport. It supplied the local naval base with fresh produce, dairy products, and poultry. During the war years Jackie picked fruit, fed chickens—her least favorite chore because she found the birds mean—milked cows, and collected eggs.

For part of each summer, Jackie and Lee would still go back to East Hampton to spend time with their father and grandfather. Now in her mid-teens, Jackie attracted attention from local boys, but she was uninterested. She preferred the company of older men, like a Russian aristocrat she met in the summer of 1944. Her cousins noticed that although Jackie was still prone to being a loner, she also seemed more self-assured and had developed a droll sense of humor. Black Jack noticed, too. He had already been angry and resentful at having to share Jackie with Hughdie. But watching his daughter mature into a woman pained Jack because he was losing his little girl and would never get her back.

SHE SAID . . .

"I always love it so at Merrywood—so peaceful—with the river and the dogs. I will never know which I love best— Hammersmith with its green fields and summer winds—or Merrywood in the snow—with the river and those great steep hills. I love them both—whichever I'm at—just as passionately as I loved the one behind."

THEY SAID . . .

"It was a peaceful, golden life . . . a world of deliberate quietude removed from twentieth-century tension. It was a life that gave total security, but not much preparation for the real world. Most of us broke away. Jackie surely rejected the Great Lady tradition. But we all in one way or another have tried to re-create Merrywood's heavenly ambience in our own households."

—Gore Vidal, in *Jacqueline Bouvier Kennedy Onassis*

Education

In the 1930s, it was expected that the goal of socially prominent women was to marry well, have children, entertain guests, and oversee the staff of their various homes. Even so, being educated was considered an essential aspect of being well rounded, sophisticated—and marriageable. Career women were still relatively few in number. Those from prominent families who did pursue careers usually drifted into traditionally female professions such as teaching or channeled their career drives into charitable work with the Junior League. From a young age, Jackie looked forward to being a professional woman, entertaining the idea of being a writer or even an architect.

QUESTION

What is the Junior League?

The Junior League is a volunteer organization founded in 1901 by Mary Harriman to improve the living conditions of New York's immigrant population. Mary, the daughter of Union Pacific Railroad chairman E. H. Harriman, was a nineteen-year-old college student when she started the group with eighty other young women. Today there are more than 290 Junior Leagues in North America and the United Kingdom.

Miss Chapin's

After Jackie finished kindergarten, the Bouviers enrolled her in Miss Chapin's on East End Avenue in New York. Janet had also attended the school. When Jackie started first grade, the school had nearly 400 students and was considered the smartest school for girls in Manhattan. The day began with the entire school reciting a verse from the Bible. Any display of bad manners or inappropriate behavior would result in a trip to the headmistress's office.

In addition to their academic curriculum, which focused heavily on history, Chapin girls were taught the poise and personal character deemed integral for future society ladies. They were also instructed in practical matters, such as managing servants, handling trust funds, and making investments. In a concession to the times, Miss Chapin's School offered athletics as well as the opportunity to participate in student government. Jackie's father paid the steep $575 annual tuition, which included lunch, books, and bus transportation to and from the school.

THEY SAID...

"She was . . . very clever, very artistic, and full of the devil. She was efficient and finished her work on time. . . . Jacqueline Bouvier was a great mischief as a young thing, with a wonderful sense of humor, sharp wit, and a keen perception that sometimes poked fun at the snobbishness of her school and sheltered environment."

—Miss Affleck, homeroom teacher, in *As We Remember Her*

Though she was a good student, Jackie misbehaved. She once received a D in Form (Chapin's version of conduct) on her report card after she was kicked out of her geography class for being disruptive.

Miss Porter's

Jackie spent six years at Chapin's, withdrawing after Janet married Hughdie and moved the family to Merrywood. For two years, starting in the autumn of 1942, Jackie attended the Holton-Arms School in Washington, D.C. When she was fifteen, Jackie left Merrywood for Miss Porter's School in Farmington, Connecticut. Located near Hartford, Miss Porter's was an exclusive boarding school. Jackie's decision to live away from home was both academic and personal. It provided her with both the independence and college preparatory curriculum she wanted.

In many ways, Jackie was a typical teenager. She had a rebellious streak, liked getting her way, and could be distant and distracted. But she was also intelligent and enjoyed participating in activities. She was an A student and was involved in the riding club, the theater, and the school newspaper.

> **FACT**
>
> Through the late 1930s, most of the top private girls' schools were essentially finishing schools. Critics charged that the emphasis on social skills over curriculum promoted class-consciousness and did not adequately prepare young women for higher education opportunities. As a result, Farmington started offering college preparatory classes in 1939.

Miss Manners

Both Miss Chapin's and Miss Porter's stressed the importance of decorum. But like any teenager, Jackie could be rebellious, self-involved, and thoughtless. After her parents' divorce, she earned a rare rebuke from her father for failing to call him as he had requested. He told her it made him feel neglected.

Jackie also was manipulative and became very adept at playing her parents against one another. To get something she wanted from Janet, Jackie would talk in glowing terms about her father. Not wanting Jack to get an upper hand when it came to their daughter's affections, Janet would give Jackie pretty much whatever she wanted. Likewise, Jackie knew how jealous her father was of Hughdie, so the slightest expression of appreciation for Auchincloss ensured that Black Jack would give his little girl anything she wanted.

> **SHE SAID . . .**
>
> "Growing up was not so hard. . . . It happened gradually over the three years I spent trying to imitate girls who had callers every Saturday. I passed the finish line when I learned to smoke in the balcony of the Normandie Theater in New York from a girl who pressed a Longfellow upon me."

At Miss Porter's, Jackie displayed her subversive side by flouting the rules. It was strictly forbidden for students to go horseback riding without specific parental permission. But after Danseuse arrived, Jackie coerced her best friend Nancy "Tucky" Tuckerman to ride the horse, even though she had never been in a saddle before. Predictably, she fell off and got hurt. But following Jackie's advice, Tucky claimed she had fallen out of a tree and both girls escaped punishment.

Like all finishing schools, Miss Porter's insisted on good table manners, from carefully modulated voices at the dinner table to proper use of silverware. The students also learned table service. Once, on a dare, Jackie dropped a slice of chocolate cream pie directly onto the lap of a teacher known for her perfectionism. Jackie put her acting talent to work and responded so apologetically the teacher never suspected it had been a prank. Likewise, none of the administration would have ever guessed it was the refined Miss Bouvier who stole fresh-baked cookies from the pantry for an after-curfew snack.

Jackie's worst habit was smoking. Janet strongly disapproved, so Jackie had to sneak around to smoke when she was at Merrywood or Hammersmith. Once when she was caught off guard, Jackie stashed her cigarette in the cushion of a couch. Janet discovered her deception when the fabric caught fire.

FACT

The ultimate authority on good manners in Jackie's day was a socialite named Emily Post. The daughter of a prominent architect, Emily's marriage to a wealthy banker ended in divorce when she was thirty-two years old. She began writing to earn money to maintain her standard of living. Her 1922 book, *Etiquette*, was a best seller and became the bible of appropriate behavior.

Debutante of the Year

America's first debutante ball, also known as a cotillion, was held in 1748 in Philadelphia when fifty-nine families presented their daughters to other members of elite society. The main point was to let it be known that the young women were of legal age and available for a suitable marriage. Things had not changed all that much when Jackie was presented—twice—in the summer of 1947. Her first introduction was a late-afternoon reception at Hammersmith attended by 300 guests whom Jackie greeted as they passed down a formal receiving line. Instead of the designer gown her mother wanted her to wear, Jackie wore a simple white dress and gloves, which hid the cigarette stains on her fingers. The reception was held in conjunction with the christening of Jackie's infant half brother James Lee Auchincloss, Janet's second child with Hughdie and her only son. Their daughter, Janet Jennings, had been born two years earlier in 1945.

Jackie's official coming out was held August 16 at Newport's Clambake Club. While she had enjoyed the reception at Hammersmith, she found the cotillion repressive. She didn't like being obligated to dance with every young man who asked or making small talk with their parents. But to observers, Jackie was the perfect debutante. Social columnist Cholly Knickerbocker named her Debutante of the Year, describing her as regal and having poise, intelligence, and the daintiness of Dresden porcelain.

Black Jack and the other Bouviers watched Jackie's coming out from a distance. The only other Bouvier relative invited to her coming out parties was her sister Lee. Janet had effectively cut her ex-husband and his family out of her life. Even though Jack's time with his daughters was limited, he continued to help support Jackie and Lee, sending them each $50 a month. Out of that, they were expected to pay for personal items such as makeup, clothes, and entertainment. It was a pittance compared to the money the Auchincloss children had access to. Jackie's cousin John Davis believes it was that feeling of being the poor relation—and Janet's example—that drew Jackie to wealthy men. There was no way Jacqueline Bouvier would marry a man of simple means.

Jackie graduated from Miss Porter's in June 1947. She won the Maria McKinney Memorial Award for Excellence in Literature. Her prize for winning was a book of Edna St. Vincent Millay's poems. As she prepared to leave the school for college, Jackie told friends that her goal was not to be a housewife.

Chapter 4

A YEAR ABROAD

From the time she was a little girl, Jackie had been a Francophile. She loved the language and the country's artistic history. Her interest in Paris's café society further influenced her desire to visit the City of Lights. The opportunity to spend a year in France gave Jackie a new sophistication and had a lasting impact on how she viewed America and the world.

Attending Vassar

After the restrictive confines of boarding school, college gave Jackie a chance to assert her independence. Her grades and college entrance exam scores were good enough to give Jackie her choice of colleges. She chose Vassar, a highly regarded women's college located eighty miles north of Manhattan in Poughkeepsie, New York, on the Hudson River. One of around two hundred incoming freshmen, she studied Shakespeare, religious history, literature, and languages. Outside of class Jackie joined the staffs of *The Vassar Miscellany News* and the art club and worked as a costume designer in the drama club. Typically, classmates remembered her as being fun to be around but extremely secretive. Her trick was to get other people to talk about their lives without revealing anything personal in return.

FACT

At the time of Jackie's admission, Vassar was one of the Seven Sisters—the name given to the elite liberal arts women's colleges on the East Coast, which also included Barnard, Bryn Mawr, Mount Holyoke, Radcliffe, Smith, and Wellesley. Founded in 1861, Vassar became coed in 1969 and remains one of the nation's top-ranked colleges.

Initially, Jackie enjoyed the freedom offered by college life, and although she was particularly enthralled with her classes—Jackie later called her Shakespeare teacher, Helen Sandison, an inspiration—she was less enamored of Poughkeepsie. She soon spent every weekend away from campus.

Dating

After her debutante season, Jackie started dating. Most of her suitors were young men attending Ivy League schools such as Harvard, Yale, or Princeton. She particularly enjoyed going to college football games. But none of the would-be beaux sustained her interest and there were seldom more than one or two dates. Her most solid relationship remained with her father. She regularly took the train into Manhattan to spend the weekend at his apartment. Sometimes she would bring friends, who would be utterly charmed by Black Jack. Ironically, most of his girlfriends during this time were only a few years older than his daughter. Rather than be upset, Jackie was pleased that so many women found her father attractive.

Jack, on the other hand, worried about having his daughters taken away by another man. Knowing it was inevitable, he did his best to keep Jackie and Lee from falling for the wrong kind of guy. He repeatedly told them that all men were rats and that it was important to always keep them guessing—and waiting. Playing hard to get would get Jackie and Lee what, and who, they wanted. His advice was decidedly on-target. The more aloof Jackie was, the more men she had trying to catch her eye. She developed a coy, flirtatious personality and adopted a soft, little-girl voice that many of her old schoolmates saw as an obvious affectation. But men were captivated. They were also invariably left frustrated. All of her flirtations were just that.

Jackie and her father,
John V. Bouvier III, 1947

*Photo Credit: Morgan
Collection/Hulton Archives/
Getty Images*

Summer Abroad

In July and August 1948, Jackie took her first trip to Europe with family friends Helen and Judy Bowdoin and Julia Bissell. The trip came about after the Bowdoins' stepfather urged Hughdie to let Jackie go, too. Janet agreed and recruited Helen Shearman, Jackie's former Latin teacher at the Holton Arms, to act as the girls' chaperone. They traveled aboard the *Queen Mary* and spent seven weeks traveling through England, France, Belgium, Switzerland, and Italy.

THEY SAID...

"She told me about the complicated relationship with her father, whom she admired and respected because women were crazy about him. She'd say to him about the mothers of some of her friends, 'What about her?' and he'd say, 'Yes, I've had her.' She thought that that was the most wonderful thing. She had all the wrong standards."

—John "Demi" Gates, in *America's Queen*

The group disembarked in Southampton, England, and took the train to London. The city was still trying to rebuild after the devastating bombings it suffered during World War II. For Jackie, it was a very moving, emotional experience. They visited the severely damaged St. Paul's Cathedral. One of the highlights of the entire trip for Jackie was meeting Winston Churchill at a Buckingham Palace garden party.

In France, they visited many museums, including the Louvre. Jackie loved being able to see in person works of art she had studied in school. She was especially enamored with the palace at Versailles, where she spoke to the guides in fluent French.

The Sorbonne

Coming back to Vassar for her sophomore year was an emotional letdown for Jackie after her exciting summer in Europe. Getting away from Poughkeepsie became her primary objective. She complained that she felt like a schoolgirl among schoolgirls on campus and considered dropping out to become a model in New York. She was bored and wanted to see more of the world. By early 1949 she was convinced she wanted to live in Europe full time.

Exchange Student

During the spring term, Jackie saw a notice on a bulletin board about a yearlong student exchange program being offered through Smith College to the Sorbonne, the University of Paris's Humanities Department. Through the intercession of a family friend, Jackie was accepted to the program. On August 23, 1949, she once again set sail for Europe.

She spent the first six weeks taking an intensive six-week French language course at the University of Grenoble, taking classes for eight hours a day. In letters home, she described the locals as happy people who spoke with a French "twang." She was enchanted with the custom called La Bénédiction de la Mer, which took place in the Camargue region. Every year when the Camargue is flooded by the Rhone River, locals ride their horses into the water and bless it. Jackie explored the countryside around Grenoble, visiting grottoes and underground rivers. She and some other students once got so wrapped up joining residents in singing and dancing one night at a quaint restaurant they missed their train and had to walk five miles back to Grenoble. In October, Jackie left for Paris to begin her studies at the Sorbonne, promising herself she would one day return.

FACT

Located in the Rhone-Alps region in southeast France, Grenoble is called the capital of the French Alps. Settled by the Romans in 43 B.C., the town was renamed Gratianopolis in 379 A.D. to honor Emperor Gratian. The university was founded in 1339, but Grenoble remained sparsely populated until the mid-nineteenth century when the first water-powered electricity plant was built nearby.

Jackie's Parisian Family

Rather than live in a dorm at the Sorbonne with the other exchange students, Jackie chose to live with a Parisian family. She and two others moved in with the Countess Guyot de Renty and her family at 76 Avenue Mozart in Paris. Madam de Renty's husband had died in a Nazi concentration camp. She shared her home with three daughters. One, Ghislaine, was divorced with a four-year-old son, Christian. Another, Claude, was Jackie's age, and the two young women became lifelong friends. Staying with the de Rentys, who spoke no English in the house, allowed Jackie to immerse herself in French culture. When she wasn't in class or studying, she explored, spending countless hours at the Louvre and taking advantage of the city's opera, theater, and ballet.

THEY SAID...

"The mood of the Parisians at that time was joyous. We were meeting friends and going around everywhere. It was [Jackie's] first time abroad alone. She discovered what it was to be alone but she was also now free to do what she wanted. The great part of that was a deeper pursuit of culture."

—Claude de Renty, in *As We Remember Her*

Jackie spent the Christmas holiday in England, visiting her father's former lover, Anne Plugge. For a while Jackie spent time with the son of a French diplomat. But she later confessed to her stepbrother Yusha that the year had been wonderful and exciting but not at all romantic. She seemed far more interested in her studies. In addition to the classes she took at the Sorbonne, Jackie also took art lessons at the École du Louvre and a class in diplomatic history at the École de Science Politique.

Paris in 1950

For most of the twentieth century, Paris was considered the artistic center of Western culture. When Jackie arrived for her year of study, parts of Paris still bore the scars of World War II. But the city leaders worked hard to re-establish Paris as Europe's premiere cultural center and soon attracted a new wave of expatriate writers and artists who brought a new excitement to the galleries, salons, and cafés.

Daily Life

Jackie quickly adapted to daily life in Paris. She explored the city on foot, walking the wide avenues lined with designer shops and out-of-the-way side streets with small, family-owned shops and produce markets. On Sundays, the Left Bank was filled with strolling locals and tourists who browsed through bookshops and ate lunch at sidewalk bistros and listened to music at one of the jazz clubs or went to a movie theater at night.

The Place St. Michel was a traditional gathering place for bohemians. On warm days, sunbathers lined the concrete banks of the Seine, and ice-cream vendors hawked their wares in front of the Louvre. Some streets, like the Rue de Rivoli, were gridlocked with cars, while other streets, hardly wider than a Madison Avenue sidewalk, were deserted except for local residents carrying packages home from the local market.

Fashion

On the Champs-Élysées, Paris's most famous and widest boulevard, or at the fashionable shops and jewelers along the Rue de la Paix, wealthy Parisian women wore the latest designer fashions. In 1950, no clothes designer was more famous than Christian Dior, whose dresses and footwear were a throwback to the glamour days of the 1920s.

World War II had had a dramatic effect on every facet of life. Traditionally, New York designers would go to Europe and attend the Parisian haute couture fashion shows before returning to America to basically copy what they had seen. But after Germany occupied Paris, designers in the United States changed their focus from high fashion to sportswear. Because natural fabrics were in short supply because of the war effort, designers also began using synthetic fibers.

FACT

During World War II, France's fashion industry went into hibernation. The country's best-known design house, Chanel, stopped production, and French *Vogue* went out of print between 1941 and 1945. To accommodate government-mandated restrictions on the amount of fabric used, styles such as double cuffs, hoods, and patch pockets were banned.

Dior was the first important designer to emerge in postwar France. His styles, which he called the "New Look," were ultra feminine, with fitted jackets worn with no blouse underneath and full skirts with sharply nipped waistlines. His extravagant use of material, after years of wartime rationing, made a bold statement of opulence. Prior to her trip to Europe, Jackie's interest in fashion was mostly functional—with her broad shoulders, muscular legs, and a small bosom, she dressed to hide what she considered a flawed body. But her time in Paris made her more appreciative of sophisticated designs and more conscious of her own developing style. Once again, she was frustrated by not having enough money to indulge in shopping, further instilling her determination to one day have enough money to buy whatever she wanted.

Paris Café Society

Jackie first became interested in Paris's café society history when she was a student at Miss Porter's and learned about French poet and writer Juliette de Récamier. Born in 1777, de Récamier was only fifteen when her parents forced her to marry a wealthy banker who was much older than she was. Unfulfilled by her marriage, Juliette started Paris's café society when she opened a salon that became a popular place for France's literati and political elite to meet, drink absinthe, and share ideas. Jackie was drawn to de Récamier's intelligence, independence, and devotion to the arts and felt a spiritual kinship with her.

SHE SAID . . .

"I remember last summer when we were here—I thought Paris was all glamour and glitter and rush—but of course it isn't. . . . I do love Paris and am so happy here but it is not the dazzled adoration for it I had the first time I saw it—a much more easy going and healthy affection this time."

Between the end of World War I and the start of the Great Depression, the most popular cafés were located in the Left Bank neighborhood called Montparnasse. Dôme was frequented mostly during the day and was a favorite breakfast spot. The writer Ezra Pound spent afternoons at Dôme playing chess. Matisse, the famous Impressionist painter, was also a Dôme regular, as was Picasso, who would doodle on napkins and sometimes on the tablecloths.

After World War II there was a shift away from Montparnasse to cafés along the Boulevard Saint-Germain. The two most popular were Les Deux Magots and its nearby rival, Café de Flore. Philosophers and life partners Jean-Paul Sartre and Simone de Beauvoir relaxed at Les Deux while the Flore attracted artists such as Salvador Dalí and Joan Miró. But their notoriety also made them popular tourist destinations, driving most of the noted patrons away by the time Jackie spent her year in Paris.

French Art and the Louvre

France has a rich art history, from the prehistoric cave paintings of Lascaux to some of the most important movements in modern art, including Impressionism, Fauvism, Art Nouveau, and Surrealism.

The center of this history is Paris, which, at the time of Jackie's visit, was home to unparalleled museums, art schools, and galleries.

The École des Beaux-Arts

The École des Beaux-Arts has been one of Europe's top art schools for centuries. Founded in 1648 as the Académie des Beaux-Arts, the public institution is still one of the most prestigious schools in Europe. Located across the street from the Louvre, it boasts a strong collection of its own.

> **FACT**
>
> The most important art event in the Western world during the eighteenth and nineteenth centuries was the Salon de Paris, the official exhibition of the École des Beaux-Arts. The Salon was so influential it was practically impossible for an artist to become successful without its support.

The architecture program attracted students from all over the world. American graduates of the school would go on to design many famous buildings, including the Boston Public Library, Boston Museum of Fine Arts, Grand Central Terminal, and the Metropolitan Museum of Art.

The painting curriculum was rigid, and all students had to study drawing in a very specific order—first engravings, then plastic casts, and finally using live nude models. Only after they mastered those skills were they allowed to begin painting.

Attending the École des Beaux-Arts was an important step in becoming a profes-

SHE SAID . . .

"I loved it more than any year of my life. Being away from home gave me a chance to look at myself with a jaundiced eye. I learned not to be ashamed of a real hunger for knowledge, something I had always tried to hide, and I came home . . . with a love for Europe that I am afraid will never leave me."

sional artist; because the school prided itself on accepting only the most promising students, its entrance exam was extremely difficult. Aspiring artists prepared for the exam by studying with established artists. Today the École Nationale Supérieure des Beaux-Arts has an enrollment of around 500 students.

SHE SAID . . .

"Newport . . . I knew I didn't want the rest of my life to be there. I didn't want to marry any of the young men I grew up with—not because of them but because of their life. I didn't know what I wanted. I was still floundering."

THEY SAID . . .

"For her, French culture meant mostly French art. She had been in Washington and New York . . . however, she realized that nothing was comparable to what she would see there in French museums. She realized France was the place where she could see the best of the arts she loved—even of Italian and German and Dutch."

—Claude de Renty, in *As We Remember Her*

Louvre

The center of Paris's artistic culture is the Louvre, the most visited museum in the world. The original structure was built on the banks of the Seine in the twelfth century as a fortress to protect Paris, then Europe's largest city, from invasion. Later, it became a royal palace for Philip II. Some of the halls are so big that the King used to ride his horse through them.

In 1791, after the French Revolution toppled the monarchy, the Louvre and the adjacent Tuileries Palace were designated national palaces where important works of art and science would be housed. Two years later, the Louvre opened as a public museum. Since then, the museum has undergone numerous additions and redesigns, becoming a complex series of connected galleries and buildings.

Adventures

In February 1950, Janet and Hughdie traveled to Paris to take Jackie on a vacation during her school break. The time they spent together was tense. Janet was upset Jackie was not keeping her sights on finding a suitable husband, Hughdie complained about how expensive everything was in France, and Jackie tried overly hard to show how mature and independent she was.

At Jackie's suggestion, Hughdie readily agreed that they travel coach on their three-week trip to Vienna, Salzburg, and Munich. She felt too isolated in first class and thought it was more fun and interesting to sit next to strangers and hear their stories. Being a history buff, she wanted to see a Nazi concentration camp. The experience was traumatic and emotional. Her cousin John Davis said that Jackie did not blame Germans in general for the atrocities. She blamed the Nazis, whom she saw as a distinct group.

Road Trip

Jackie finished her term at the Sorbonne in May, saying she had never worked so hard in school. As a reward, she took a road trip with Claude de Renty through the south of France, visiting medieval castles and quaint villages, including Pont Saint-Esprit, the Bouvier ancestral home. Living like Bohemians, Jackie and Claude washed their clothes in streams, picnicked in picturesque woods, and stayed in quaint hotels or with de Renty cousins. They ended up in St. Jean de Luz, a seaside resort near the Spanish border where they stayed at a chateau with several other young Americans from Jackie's social circle, including "Demi" Gates, who eventually became a friend after she turned down his repeated romantic advances.

Jackie met up with Yusha in Paris. In no hurry to go home and spend the rest of the summer with Janet and Hughdie in Newport, she had convinced him to spend August traveling with her through England, Scotland, and Ireland, beginning with the Dublin Horse Show. Using Auchincloss connections, they were invited to have lunch at the American embassy and were given an embassy car and chauffeur for sightseeing. The chauffeur later took them to his local pub where the owner introduced Jackie to Guinness. The next day they met with the prime minister and completed their stay in Dublin by seeing a George Bernard Shaw play at the Abbey Theatre. From there they drove to Limerick and visited a former Auchincloss cook who had retired back to Ireland and lived in a thatched cottage. Jackie also visited Cork, the Lees' ancestral home. She was so charmed by Ireland and its people she didn't want to leave.

They toured castles in Scotland and attended the Edinburgh arts festival before heading to London, where they spent time sightseeing before boarding the *Liberté* and sailing for home. It was late August by the time they docked in New York. Jackie's year abroad was officially over.

Lasting Impressions

Spending a year in Europe had a profound impact on Jackie. Out from under the constant watchful eye of her mother, Jackie blossomed intellectually and emotionally. She immersed herself in the city's rich artistic culture, developing a deep appreciation for all the performance arts. Even though she had some American roommates with the de Rentys, Jackie lived as a Parisian—stopping for a glass of wine on the way home from the Sorbonne, eating a quiet dinner at a local boîte, reading the newspaper while sipping espresso at the neighborhood café. Adapting to the city's pace gave Jackie a new layer of sophistication that boosted her confidence, at least superficially.

Money Issues

Jackie loved Merrywood, but she didn't want her mother's stuffy lifestyle with Hughdie. She wanted a more worldly existence where she could pursue her intellectual interests. But she didn't want to worry about paying for it.

Jackie became increasingly concerned with financial security after Grampy Jack Bouvier died in 1948. To the family's surprise, he died with a lot less money than anyone expected. He had spent much of his fortune on the family's lavish lifestyle at Lasata and in New York. All that was left of his many millions was $800,000. After inheritance taxes, that amount dwindled considerably. Jackie and Lee, along with all the other cousins, received a total inheritance of $3,000. Jackie felt especially chagrined knowing that Hughdie's children, including her half siblings, had all been set up with trust funds by the Auchincloss family. She and Lee were left to fend for themselves.

Unable to afford its upkeep, the Bouviers were forced to sell Lasata in April 1950 for a mere $40,000. It was the end of an era. For Jackie it was just another confirmation: To live in the style to which she was accustomed, to have the freedom to travel to Europe, to afford the wonderful clothes she saw along the Rue de la Paix, to indulge her passion for the arts, she needed to have money—and a lot of it. It wouldn't come from an inheritance, so Jackie knew before long it would be time to start looking for a wealthy husband.

Chapter 5

AN INDEPENDENT STREAK

As Jackie prepared for life after college, she found herself pulled in opposite directions. Part of her needed the financial security of great wealth, but she objected to being another debutante biding time until a suitable marriage proposal came along. So Jackie exerted her independence and joined the work force.

Leaving Vassar

While Jackie was in Europe, Black Jack underwent a cataract operation. When Jackie returned to New York her father was depressed. He wanted her to live with him and promised to get her a job on Wall Street after she graduated. In the past, Jackie would have been more mindful of her father's needs, but now that she was a mature woman she had her own interests and future to look after. Although she promised to consider his offer, Jackie had no desire to finish college at Vassar. After living with the de Rentys in the heart of Paris, the thought of going back to an all-girls dorm in Poughkeepsie was unbearable.

Janet had her own reasons for not wanting Jackie to go back to Vassar. She was still competitive with Jack over their children's time, attention, and affection. Janet didn't like the idea of Jackie moving in with her ex-husband, and she liked the idea of her getting a job on Wall Street even less because she feared it would give Jack that much more influence over Jackie. So Janet and Hughdie suggested Jackie live at Merrywood and finish her degree at George Washington University. Jackie agreed.

George Washington University

Located four blocks from the White House, George Washington University was the top-ranked college in Washington, known for its social sciences and international affairs programs. Jackie sent in her application late, but Janet was able to persuade the admissions dean to accept the transfer for her final two semesters of college. Jackie switched her major to French literature. In the classes students were allowed to write assignments in English, but Jackie insisted on writing all her assignments in French. She also took jour-

SHE SAID . . .

"I flatter myself on being able at times to walk out of the house looking like a poor man's Paris copy but often my mother will run up to inform me that my left stocking seam is crooked or the right-hand topcoat button about to fall off. This, I realize, is the Unforgivable Sin."

nalism and creative writing classes. A story she wrote for Muriel McClanahan's advanced composition class, titled "In Florence," was read during a broadcasted ceremony held at the university.

Jackie made an impression on her classmates, who remember her as being striking and dignified. Her aloofness kept most of her peers from approaching. Most of the friends she made were slightly older, and Jackie attended their Georgetown dinner parties. Her love life remained stalled, prompting one friend, Charles Bartlett, to pester Jackie about coming over for dinner so he could introduce her to a young man he was sure she would find interesting. Jackie politely put him off.

FACT
George Washington was a longtime advocate for a federal university in the nation's capital. After his death, a group of investors led by a Baptist missionary bought the forty-seven acres on which the new college was built. On February 9, 1821, Congress chartered Columbian College. The name was changed to George Washington University in 1904.

In later years, very little evidence of her time at George Washington University remained. All of her student documentation mysteriously disappeared around the time John Kennedy was named the Democratic nominee for president. She never attended any class reunions or spoke much of her years there, effectively cutting it out of her personal history.

Vogue's Prix de Paris Writing Contest

While Jackie was still in France, Janet came across an article in *Vogue* about its Prix de Paris contest for college seniors and gave it to Jackie. The winner would first spend six months in the magazine's Paris office working as a junior editor, then six months working on writing assignments for the New York office. Her year in Paris had inspired Jackie to pursue a writing career, so in the autumn of

1950, Jackie entered the Prix. The competition was stiff; more than 1,250 other young women from 225 colleges across the country also submitted applications.

FACT

Jackie isn't the only celebrated participant of the Prix de Paris contest. Other entrants have included interior designer Iris Barrel Apfel and authors Janet Halliday Ervin and Carole Nelson. Writer Joan Didion began her literary career in 1956 after winning the Prix's first prize.

The contest's requirements were rigorous. Participants were required to submit a layout for an entire issue of the magazine, four technical articles on high fashion, an essay about "People I Wish I Had Known," and a personal profile. In her profile, Jackie described herself as being tall with a square face. She noted that her eyes are so far apart that it took three weeks to have a pair of glasses made with a bridge wide enough to fit over her nose. She described her figure in self-deprecating terms but said she could look slim by picking the right clothes.

Jackie expressed her ambivalence with Vassar, while in the same breath admitting she regretted not studying harder and spending so many weekends away from campus. She listed her hobbies as riding, fox hunting, going to art exhibits, and painting but claimed she didn't work at any of them consistently. Jackie's cousin John Davis later suggested it was what Jackie didn't include in her profile that was most telling to those who knew her. Her family was kept firmly in the background, so much so she never mentioned her life in East Hampton or Newport. The one mention of her mother shows her as being critical and superficial.

In her second essay Jackie had to name the three people she would have most liked to know. She chose to write about poet Charles Baudelaire; playwright, poet, and novelist Oscar Wilde, and ballet producer and impresario Serge Diaghilev. Although the men were in different fields, had different backgrounds, and came from different countries, Jackie believed they shared the genius of creative idealism and insight.

Creative Eye Rewarded

Jackie's proposed issue revealed her romantic side. Using the theme "Nostalgia," she evoked what she termed a bygone era represented by images from the 1920s—Janet and Black Jack's heyday. Her imaginative marketing campaign for a new perfume compared the scent to wine—both were intoxicating liquids. She also included an illustrated layout with the perfume bottle front designed to resemble a wine label.

The judges were impressed. In April 1951 Jackie was named one of the finalists and invited to New York to attend a special dinner held in honor of the finalists. Because of final exams, Jackie couldn't attend but went to New York in early May to meet *Vogue's* editor-in-chief, Edna Woolman Chase. Less than two weeks later, Jackie was announced the Prix winner. The magazine planned to run a story about Jackie in its August 15, 1951, issue and wanted to know how soon Jackie could move to Paris to begin her internship.

THEY SAID...

"I didn't want her to go. She had already had a year in Europe and had fallen in love with Paris and I was afraid that if she returned there, she would become an expatriate. I hoped I could persuade her to turn the prize down."

—Janet Auchincloss, in *Jacqueline Bouvier Kennedy Onassis*

In the end, Jackie's tenure at *Vogue* proved short. On her first day of training in the New York office, she quit abruptly. According to John Davis, Janet was the driving force behind Jackie's decision. She undermined Jackie's confidence by openly expressing her doubt that Jackie could be a successful professional in Paris. That pressure combined with Jackie's wavering self-confidence effectively and successfully torpedoed the opportunity. But at least one *Vogue* editor believed Jackie had made the right decision. Carole Phillips found Jackie to be insecure about her abilities. Her advice to Jackie was to go back to Washington, D.C., because that's where all the eligible bachelors were.

Suitors

During her final year of college Jackie casually dated a few young men but was underwhelmed. She claimed to be indifferent to striking looks, commenting that she'd be bored after three minutes with a male model. She didn't care if her suitor had big ears, uneven teeth or was fat, skinny, or short, as long as he possessed a keen mind. None of the men she met in college stirred her intellectual interest, much less her passion. Even though she had her sights on pursuing a writing career, Jackie must have felt a niggling pressure. In the 1950s, most women in her social circle were married within a year or so of graduating from college. Jackie hadn't even met someone she was interested in dating. Her mother—and friends—decided that made Jackie the perfect candidate for matchmaking.

FACT

Georgetown was the center for Washington, D.C.'s social elite. In the early nineteenth century, its location on the Potomac made it a major port for tobacco—and a thriving slave trade center. After the Civil War, Georgetown's black community flourished until it was forced out, replaced by the *Social Register* crowd.

The Young Congressman

After numerous attempts, Charles Bartlett and his wife Martha finally convinced Jackie to attend one of their dinner parties at their Georgetown home. The invitation wasn't innocent. Bartlett had become friends with a young congressman from Massachusetts named Jack Kennedy and thought he and Jackie would be a good match. When they were introduced, Jackie remembered once being on the same train with Jack. Jackie found Jack an interesting dinner companion but later recalled thinking that he was also a man not particularly interested in marriage.

When dinner was over, Jack walked Jackie to her car and suggested they go out for a drink. But waiting in the car for her was Jackie's current beau, John Husted. Even though Kennedy made a graceful exit, Jackie suspected it would not be her last encounter with the charismatic politician.

An Engagement to Forget

Tall, handsome, and possessing a reputation as a good dancer, John Husted came from a prominent *Social Register* family. His two sisters had attended Farmington with Jackie, and his parents knew Black Jack. When he and Jackie started dating in 1951, Black Jack was thrilled—first, because John worked on Wall Street; second, because Jackie stayed at her father's apartment when she was in New York for dates with John.

Husted was becoming serious about Jackie, and for a while she allowed herself to be swept along by his amorous pursuit. When John impulsively proposed in early 1952, Jackie accepted. The engagement was officially announced in the *Washington Times-Herald* on January 21, and the couple planned a June wedding. One item glaringly missing from the article was the slightest mention of the bride-to-be's father—Janet obviously saw to it that Black Jack was shut out from his daughter's engagement announcement.

QUESTION

What happened to the *Washington Times-Herald*?

The *Times-Herald* was formed in 1939 when the *Washington Times* merged with the *Washington Herald*. In 1954 the paper was bought by its liberal rival, the *Washington Post*, becoming the *Washington Post & Times-Herald*. By the early 1970s, *Times-Herald* was removed from the masthead.

Within weeks of announcing their engagement, Jackie had second thoughts. Her sister Lee believed some of the misgivings filtered down from their mother. Although the Husteds were socially prominent, Janet considered John average. It was also clear that Jackie wasn't passionate about him. The couple's engagement party at Merrywood was noticeably subdued, and Jackie openly expressed her doubts to friends. She envisioned her life as John's wife being calm but dull. She wanted more. In mid-March 1952, John spent the weekend at Merrywood. Before he left to return to New York, Jackie returned the engagement ring. The marriage was off.

Striking Out on Her Own

The summer after her graduation, Jackie took another trip to Europe, this time with her sister, Lee. They kept a detailed, humorous journal called *One Special Summer* that also included Jackie's poems and illustrations. Traveling without chaperones, the sisters faithfully recorded every adventure. Through Hughdie's family connections, they met ambassadors, aristocrats, artists, intellectuals, and a cast of eccentric characters, including their cabin mate on the trip across the Atlantic. The ninety-something woman liked sleeping in the nude and kept the girls awake by turning her light on and off all night.

The person who had the greatest impact on Jackie was noted art critic Bernard Berenson, whom they visited at his home in Tuscany. She considered him as wise about life as he was insightful about art.

Jackie took art lessons in Venice and bought a second-hand car in London so she

SHE SAID . . .

"It was the difference between living and existing that he had spoken of, and both of us [Jackie and Lee] had simply been existing in our selfish ways far too long. 'The only way to exist happily is to love your work,' he said. 'Anything you want, you must make enemies and suffer for.'"

and Lee could drive into the countryside. In Spain they were invited to a party thrown by local aristocrats who lived in a converted monastery. Jackie sat in a chair that once belonged to Christopher Columbus and admired their collection of royal jewels and handwritten notes from King George V. Jackie later wryly noted that their hosts' sons were only interested in getting Jackie and Lee to jitterbug with them.

When the sisters returned from Europe in September, Jackie was overcome with a restless malaise. Even her beloved Merrywood seemed confining. Janet's suggestion was for Jackie to find a wealthy husband who could give her the financial means to continue traveling and furthering her interest in art.

FACT

In the 1950s, social conservatives pushed "traditional" families where the men were the sole earners. Those women who did work until marriage usually gravitated toward low-level clerical jobs. Teaching was also an "acceptable" profession. It was less common for women to break into traditionally male-dominated professions such as medicine, law, and engineering, although some women did.

Jackie had other ideas. She wanted to be in the center of things and was more determined than ever to pursue writing as a career. It wasn't simple personal ambition that drove her. She resented the high-society notion that a woman's accomplishments were measured by whom she married. She wanted to feel as if she was accomplishing something useful. She also needed the extra money. The relatively small allowance from Black Jack barely covered her personal expenses. So Jackie asked Hughdie's friend Arthur Krock to put in a good word for her at the *Washington Times-Herald*, which was known for employing young women out of college. Krock did, and Jackie was hired as a part-time receptionist. But as usual, she had bigger plans for herself.

The "Inquiring Camera Girl"

Editor-in-Chief Frank Waldrop was impressed with Jackie's straight-forward personality and obvious intelligence. But when she made it clear she wanted to be an active member of the newspaper business, not just someone answering phones, Waldrop was skeptical. He bluntly asked Jackie if she was serious about journalism or simply biding time until someone proposed to her. She assured him she genuinely wanted to write, and Waldrop promised to consider her request.

Shortly before Christmas in 1951, Waldrop came up with what he considered a perfect vehicle for Jackie. The Inquiring Photographer had been a regular column in the *Washington Times-Herald* for years. The premise was to pose a topical question to people then run their responses and pictures. Up to then, the column had always been shot and written by a male reporter. But Waldrop thought he might shake things up by having Jackie do it. At the time, it was a daring move in the male-dominated newspaper business. But if nothing else, it would have people talking.

Jackie had never used a professional camera before, but she proved a quick study and after just a couple of days was able to take usable headshots. The new column was called Inquiring Camera Girl. She was paid $42.50 a week. After three months Jackie was given a byline on the column.

The assignment gave her the freedom to tackle any topic and approach people from all walks of life. Her questions reflected both a subversive humor and a sharp intelligence. Some questions were whimsical: Would you like to be famous? Some were

SHE SAID . . .

"One of my most annoying faults is getting very enthusiastic over something at the beginning and then tiring of it halfway through. I am trying to counteract this by not getting too enthusiastic over too many things at once. . . . I want above all to become a working girl who earns her own living."

based in the culture of the time: If you found out your spouse was a former Communist, what would you do? Others reflected Jackie's own subtle feminism: When did you discover women are not the weaker sex?

She spoke to average citizens on the street as well as senators and socialites. For the next year and a half, Jackie proved she was more than just a sheltered socialite. She was an independent woman capable of supporting herself.

The Congressman from Massachusetts

Through her work at the paper Jackie met some of Washington's brightest up-and-coming young people, but none of the men she met piqued her interest. Yusha became her most constant companion, and Jackie sometimes wondered out loud if she would remain single the rest of her life. Her old friend Charlie Bartlett was determined to see she didn't. Bartlett had never approved of her engagement to Husted, thinking they were an ill-matched pair. Instead, Charlie believed Jackie was the perfect match for Jack Kennedy.

> ## THEY SAID...
> "I just thought she was a girl with extraordinary promise . . . and really a sort of basic joie de vivre. It seemed to me that she'd be a marvelous wife for just anybody. But it had to be someone with a lot of sophistication. And I knew our friend Jack was running around—I thought it would be good for him."
>
> —Charlie Bartlett, in *America's Queen*

During the winter of 1951, Jackie and Lee vacationed with Janet and Hughdie in Palm Beach, Florida. Charlie, who owned a home there, orchestrated for Jackie a visit to the Kennedys, who lived nearby. Jack's mother, Rose, was not present, but Joe, the family patriarch immediately took a liking to Jackie. However, with a house full of Kennedys, visitors, and political advisors, her encounter with Jack was hardly intimate.

In May 1952, the Bartletts hosted another dinner. Martha called Jackie and mentioned she was short a male guest. She casually suggested Jackie invite Congressman Kennedy. It was almost a year to the day from when they had first been introduced at the Bartlett's previous dinner party. Jack, a few weeks shy of his thirty-fifth birthday, was now running for the Senate. He had also recently been voted America's most eligible bachelor.

FACT

John Kennedy's Republican opponent in the 1952 Massachusetts senatorial race was Henry Cabot Lodge Jr. Lodge had been elected in 1936 and served until 1944 when he resigned in order to enlist in the army during World War II. He was the first senator since the Civil War to go on active military duty. He was re-elected in 1946.

Jackie was very attracted to Jack but was initially wary of getting seriously involved. He was an independent man who hadn't seemed interested in settling down. He also had a reputation for being a ladies' man—although not even his friends knew the extent of his sexual relationships—and Jackie was still insecure about her own appeal. Plus, he was already a well-known public figure, which would mean giving up a large chunk of her personal privacy. On the other hand, Jackie was also known to be attracted to "dangerous" men, like her father. When it became clear at dinner that night at the Bartlett's that Jack was smitten with Jackie, she suspected that their romance was about to begin in earnest.

Chapter 6

THE KENNEDYS

The Kennedys—America's royalty. Powerful, rich, and influential, they are regarded by their admirers as dedicated citizens committed to the public good through their political service, philanthropy, and social consciousness. To their critics, they are the spoiled, law-evading scions of a corrupt patriarch whose ambition was matched only by his ruthlessness. Regardless of one's view, there's no denying that the Kennedy family story embodies the best and worst of the American dream: self-made immigrants whose successes and achievements have been repeatedly tempered by tragedies of Shakespearean proportions.

Ambition in Their Blood

In 1848, a beleaguered farmer named Patrick Kennedy emigrated from Ireland during the Great Potato Famine. He made his home in Boston and started a family, but he died of cholera in 1858, the same year his son Patrick Joseph, or P. J., was born. Patrick's widow, Bridget, never remarried. Instead she supported P. J. and her three daughters with single-minded determination. She worked for a while as a shop clerk, then later as a hairdresser. Eventually Bridget co-owned a small shop that sold sewing supplies. Bridget's daughters helped out by looking after their little brother while he attended school at the Sisters of Notre Dame.

FACT
The great Irish potato famine began in September 1845 when previously healthy potato plants began to rot in the ground. It was later determined that an airborne fungus brought to the United Kingdom from North America was responsible. An estimated one million Irish—one out of every nine—died in the 1840s as a result of the famine.

A Working Man

When P. J. turned fourteen, Bridget told him it was time to start working, and he got a job as a packer at the East Boston Shipyards. Like his mother, P. J. was careful with his money. He lived simply and saved as much as he could. With the help of his mother and sisters, he was able to buy a dilapidated tavern in a seedy Boston neighborhood. Although he did not drink, P. J. knew that bars were an integral part of Boston's immigrant culture. The saloon made enough money for P .J. to buy another. Both prospered, and Kennedy became a well-known figure in Boston. In 1885, he established P. J. Kennedy and Company, a wholesale liquor import business. That same year he decided to run for political office and was elected to the Massachusetts State Assembly.

A Family Man

In 1887, P.J. married Mary Augusta Hickey, the daughter of a prosperous businessman in the city. They lived in a large town house in East Boston, where they started a family. A son, Joseph Patrick Kennedy, was born in 1888, and two daughters followed. P. J. served six years as an assemblyman before running for the State Senate. He won easily. His import business was making so much money that in 1895 he cofounded a bank, the Columbia Trust Company. He and Mary moved out of East Boston and into a mansion near the city's financial district. He employed a large staff who tended to the wants and desires of his family. It was in this environment of privilege that P. J.'s son, Joseph Patrick Kennedy, grew up.

Even though he was respected and successful, P. J. never forgot his humble beginnings. He instilled a furious work ethic in his son and made it clear that anything less than first place amounted to failure. Young Joseph took his father's lessons to heart. As a teenager he spent every spare minute dreaming up new ways to earn money. He hawked newspapers, did go-fer work at his father's bank, and sold snacks to dockworkers. He even ran errands for Orthodox Jews on Saturday when their faith prohibited them from working on their own. Joseph was determined to make his father proud by becoming even more successful than P. J.

FACT

East Boston was originally five unconnected islands—Noddle, Hog, Governor's, Bird, and Apple—that were joined through landfill in the early nineteenth century. The area was home to a succession of Boston's diverse immigrant population, alternately Irish, Jewish, Italian, and now Latino. In the 1850s, East Boston was a well-regarded shipbuilding site and today is home to Logan International Airport.

The Outsider

P. J. and Mary wanted the best for their son. When he was thirteen they enrolled him in the prestigious Boston Latin School, a main training ground for future Harvard students. Joseph was one of the few Catholics at the Protestant school. Although he got along with his classmates and was even elected class president, he struggled in his class work. He had good instincts and street smarts, but academics were often beyond him. He was proficient in mathematics, but he was unable to master advanced subjects such as geometry. After failing physics, Latin, and French in his junior year, he was forced to repeat the grade. Joseph's difficulties in school made him all the more determined to prove he would be a success.

Harvard Bound

Like his father, Joseph did not drink alcohol. In fact, his favorite beverage was milk. He eschewed coffee and cigarettes as well. When he graduated from Boston Latin, his goal was simple: to be rich. But his parents insisted he go to college first. He applied to Harvard, considered the best Ivy League school. Despite his mediocre grades, Joe was accepted—partly because of family connections but also because of his perceived potential. P. J.'s son just seemed destined to be an important man. The fact that he was also the leading hitter in Boston's high school baseball league didn't hurt, either.

QUESTION

What is the Ivy League?

Originally, the Ivy League referred to the athletic conference comprised of Brown, Columbia, Cornell, Dartmouth, Harvard, Princeton, the University of Pennsylvania, and Yale. The term has since come to represent the schools' academic reputations. All are ranked among the top colleges and universities in the world. All but Cornell were founded prior to the Revolutionary War.

Not surprisingly, Joe also struggled academically at Harvard. To make sure he graduated, he chose musical appreciation as his major. Throughout his college career, Joe never stopped making money. He and his friend Joe Donovan bought a used bus for $600 and started a sightseeing business during summer vacations. They sold tickets at the city's main railroad terminal for excursions to the historical sites at Lexington and Concord, where the first battles of the Revolutionary War were fought. Selling tickets required a permit, which P. J. made sure his son received.

Joe's college experience further inflamed his determination to succeed. Initially, Joe enjoyed his life at Harvard, assuming he would be as accepted there as he had been at Boston Latin. But he soon learned that Catholics were not always welcome into the elite clubs that many of his friends belonged to. It was a devastating experience that informed the rest of his life.

THEY SAID...

"For the first time . . . he understood what being a Catholic in Boston meant: he would perpetually be an outsider. And he later said . . . that night, when all of his friends got into this fancy . . . club, and he was denied entrance, he looked at himself in a different way. From then on he realized he was going to have to fight that world."

—Doris Kearns Goodwin, in *America's Queen*

Business Savvy

When Joe Kennedy graduated from Harvard, he promised his friends he'd be a millionaire by the time he was thirty-five. As usual, P. J. paved the way. In 1912 he got his son hired as a bank examiner for the state of Massachusetts. The job gave Joe access to confidential information about the banks' financial holdings and business plans. He used this information to buy and sell stocks for personal gain—what today would be called insider trading, a federal offense. He invested $1,000 in an investment company called Old Colony Realty Associates that took over the mortgages on homes that had defaulted—again, information obtained while he was a state examiner. He would cosmetically fix up the houses with a coat of paint, then resell them for significant profits. When he dissolved the company, he had made more than $75,000 off his initial investment.

Joe's Smuggling Past

In January 1914, Joe was named president of Columbia Trust, making him the youngest bank president in the country. In October of that same year he married Rose Fitzgerald, daughter of Boston mayor John Francis Fitzgerald, the first son of Irish immigrants elected mayor in America. Fitzgerald and P. J. were the two most influential men in Boston, and the union of their children cemented their power base. Joe Kennedy would unabashedly use those family connections to further his personal and political ambitions. He would use less savory associates to get rich.

THEY SAID...

"Joe's time was his own, as it had been and always would be. School and college had once taken much of it before, and now it was business that did so. . . . We were individuals with highly responsible roles in a partnership that yielded rewards which we shared."

—Rose Fitzgerald Kennedy, in *America's Queen*

Starting a Family

The Kennedys' honeymoon period was short-lived. Once settled in a new house in Brookline, Massachusetts, Joe's primary interests were making money and siring children. Rose became pregnant almost immediately and nine months later gave birth to the couple's first child, Joseph Patrick Jr. on July 25, 1915. In short order John (1917), Rosemary (1918), Kathleen (1920), Eunice (1921), Patricia (1924), Robert (1925), Jean (1928), and Edward (1932) were welcomed into the family. After Kathleen's birth, the family moved into a twelve-room house. While Joe immersed himself in business ventures and extramarital affairs, Rose was left to raise her children in relative isolation, although Joe did provide her with a sizable household staff. Lonely and dissatisfied, Rose once tried to leave her husband, but her father wouldn't hear of it and sent her back.

FACT
The Black Hand was an extortion crime gang. The typical targets were wealthy Italian immigrants. A letter would be left at their doorstep threatening bodily harm or death if the "ransom" demanded was not paid. The letter would be signed with a handprint done in black ink. The practice disappeared as more profitable rackets, such as bootlegging, emerged.

On January 29, 1919, Congress approved the Eighteenth Amendment, and the era of Prohibition began. For Joe Kennedy, it was an opportunity to make a financial windfall. There was no shortage of private citizens and speakeasies willing to pay top dollar for smuggled liquor. To facilitate his new business, Joe formed alliances with mob figures in Boston, Chicago, New York, and New Orleans. Among his associates were Frank Costello, former head of the Luciano crime family, and Diamond Joe Esposito, an extortionist and bootlegger who belonged to Chicago's notorious Black Hand. Joe would buy liquor—mostly scotch—from foreign distillers, who would deliver it at specific safe spots—areas where local police and politicians had been paid to look the other way. From there, organized crime would pick up the shipments and distribute it to their clients.

Onward and Upward
Smuggling was extremely profitable, and by the mid-1920s Joe's personal fortune was in excess of $2 million—the equivalent of more than $15 million in today's money. But the size of his bank account did not bring Joe the respect and acceptance he so desperately desired. Instead, he was viewed by many as a swindler

at best and an outright criminal at worst. When his membership to the Cohasset Country Club was rejected, Joe moved his family to Riverdale in Bronx County, New York, partly to be closer to Manhattan and partly because he believed the Boston area was an inappropriate place to raise his children.

He used the fortune made from smuggling to continue playing the stock market and to invest in the film industry. While in Hollywood, he had a very public affair with actress Gloria Swanson. Rose's response was to ignore the press reports, indulge in lavish shopping trips, and go on extended vacations, leaving her children in the care of household help.

Joe may have been a philandering husband, but he was a savvy businessman. He made another $5 million in Hollywood by cofounding RKO Studio then selling off his share. He also pulled most of his money out of the stock market in early 1929. He was one of the very few who made money after the devastating stock market crash in October. As it became clear that Prohibition would be repealed, Joe made deals to open a legitimate liquor import business. He would later go on to earn an estimated $100 million during World War II in various real estate ventures.

The Ambassador

In 1938, President Franklin Roosevelt named Joseph Kennedy ambassador to Great Britain. The appointment heightened Joseph's profile, and he moved his family to London. As ambassador, Joseph argued for appeasing Nazi Germany and opposed U.S. aid to Britain after Britain entered World War II. In 1940, a *Boston Globe* reporter published some remarks Joseph had thought he made off the record. The interview showed Joseph's negative outlook on Britain's chances against the advancing Nazis, and it included some uncomplimentary comments about both the British government and First Lady Eleanor Roosevelt.

> ## THEY SAID...
> "I'm willing to spend all I've got left to keep us out of the war. There's no sense in our getting in. We'd just be holding the bag. . . . Democracy is finished in England. It may be here."
>
> —Joseph Kennedy, in remarks made to reporters, November 1940

Joseph had already handed in his resignation as ambassador, but the resulting furor ended his hopes for attaining high political office in the future. However, his time as an ambassador had provided valuable experiences for his family. His son Jack used Joseph's connections to research his senior thesis at Harvard, which he subsequently published as *Why England Slept.*

The Kennedy Curse

Every family has its share of tragedies, but the perception that tragedy haunts the Kennedys has given rise to the legend of the Kennedy curse. That their grief is usually played out in public has fueled the mystique. Some critics believe it is karmic retribution for Joe's sometimes ruthless rise to the top. Others see the Kennedys as Shakespearean figures—that great and lasting legacies often come with a terrible price.

Rosemary Kennedy

The eldest Kennedy daughter, Rosemary, called Rosie, was born with a mild form of retardation. As a child, she was shy but happy. She enjoyed going to the opera and buying clothes. But as Rosie entered adolescence, she became more aggressive and suffered from violent mood swings. It became increasingly difficult to control her, so Joe and Rose sent her to live at a convent, where she continued her education. But she would frequently sneak out and her parents worried that she would get pregnant or hurt without constant supervision.

In 1941, when Rosie was twenty-three, Joe consented to have a lobotomy performed on her. Dr. Walter Freeman and his partner Dr. James Watt convinced Joe that the procedure would reduce her violent mood swings and give her an overall calmer demeanor. At the time of Rosie's procedure, Freeman had no formal surgical training, nor did he believe in working in a sterile environment.

The lobotomy completely incapacitated Rosie. She was left incontinent, unable to verbally communicate, and in need of round-the-clock care. Freeman and Walter had turned her into little more than a human vegetable. Rosie spent her life in institutions with little overall contact with her family, except for regular visits from her sister Eunice, who founded the Special Olympics in honor of her sister. She died in 2005 at the age of 86. Hers was the first natural death among Joe and Rose's children.

FACT

Freeman and Watts also performed a lobotomy on Tennessee Williams's sister, with similarly disastrous results. Eventually, after he had performed more than 3,000 "ice pick" lobotomies, in which he inserted an ice pick into the brain through the patient's eye socket, Freeman's theories were discredited, and lobotomies went the way of blood-letting.

Joseph Kennedy Jr.

Joe Kennedy Jr. put his law studies on hold and enlisted in the navy at the start of World War II. After completing training as a pilot, he was stationed in England. Joe went on two tours of duty. He had completed his required twenty-five missions and was eligible to return home when he volunteered for one last mission on August 12, 1944. It was a dangerous secret mission intended to destroy German rocket launch sites. His plane was carrying nearly 400 boxes of high explosives when it exploded in mid-air while flying over the English Channel. He was posthumously awarded the Navy Cross, the Distinguished Flying Cross, and the Air Medal.

THEY SAID...

"It may be felt, perhaps, that Joe should not have pushed his luck so far and should have accepted his leave and come home. But two facts must be borne in mind. First, at the time of his death, he had completed probably more combat missions in heavy bombers than any other pilot of his rank in the navy and therefore was pre-eminently qualified, and secondly, as he told a friend early in August, he considered the odds at least fifty-fifty, and Joe never asked for any better odds than that."

—John F. Kennedy

Kathleen Kennedy

Kathleen Kennedy, nicknamed Kick, accompanied her father to London and took the social scene by storm. Described as beautiful and spirited, she was named the most exciting debutante of 1938. There, she met William Cavendish, Marquess of Hartington, whom she married in 1944. A month after Joe's death, Billy was killed in action by a sniper.

Kick remained in England and later became involved with an English earl named Peter Wentworth-FitzWilliam. In 1948, Kick and Peter were killed in a plane crash en route to a short holiday in Cannes. Jack was devastated. The two had forged a close bond, and her death had a lasting impact on her older brother.

Getting Involved in Politics

It was no secret that Joe Sr. had been grooming his eldest son to carry on his own shattered presidential dreams. After Joe's death, it became equally obvious that he wanted Jack to assume that role. But Jack did not have his father's burning ambition. Joe offered to buy the Brooklyn Dodgers for Jack to manage, or the *Boston Post* for Jack to run. Neither interested him.

> ## QUESTION
> **What was John F. Kennedy's experience in World War II?**
> John F. Kennedy served as the commander of a PT boat in the South Pacific during World War II. During a mission in 1943, Jack's boat was rammed by a Japanese destroyer, and Jack led his surviving crew to land. The crew was marooned for three days before being rescued. He returned home a war hero, but he also aggravated his existing back problems, which continued to plague him for the rest of his life.

Running for Congress

Jack did some freelance writing for the *Boston Globe* and for the Hearst newspapers. Although passable, his writing showed little flair and reflected his ambivalence about the profession. He was at a crossroads, unsure what direction to head. Eventually, his father made his decision for him. In 1946, Democratic congressman James Michael Curley announced his candidacy for the Boston mayoral election, and Joe decided that Jack should run for the vacant House seat. The family rented an apartment in the district to establish residency then used their name, their money, Jack's status as a war hero, and the Kennedy win-or-else work ethic to win the election.

In an ironic foreshadowing, Jack participated in a public debate over the merits of the Taft-Hartley Labor Law in 1947. His opponent: Richard Nixon, who was also a freshman congressman at the time. But overall, Kennedy's first term in office was undistinguished and uneventful. He was re-elected in 1948 and 1950, remaining popular in his district despite doing little to stand out in Congress. Jack Kennedy was more famous for his charismatic personality and family than for his political contributions.

A Run for the Senate

When Jack announced his plan to run for the Senate against Henry Cabot Lodge Jr., Joe put all of his wealth and influence into the campaign. Although Lodge was a social liberal, his father was an old hard-line Protestant—just like the people who had rejected

Joe's membership at the Cohasset Country Club. Joe loathed what the elder Lodge represented and wanted his revenge.

It was a bitter, dirty campaign, and Joe directed it. He fired Jack's campaign manager and hired his son Bobby. He made a deal with the editor of the *Boston Post* to run pro-Kennedy articles after Joe Kennedy "loaned" half a million dollars to the paper. The Kennedys spent untold amounts of money on TV ads. Jack's campaign brain trust became known as the Irish Mafia because of its campaign tactics. But Joe understood politics and made sure every member of the Kennedy family was in the public eye campaigning for Jack. It was a close race, and Jack won by less than 80,000 votes. John Kennedy's election to the Senate was truly a family victory.

> **FACT**
> Senator Joseph McCarthy, who led the House Un-American Activities Committee, once almost drowned while visiting the Kennedys' Hyannis Port estate. While sailing, he fell off the boat. John Kennedy, then a congressman, dove in the water and pulled McCarthy back to the boat.

Now that he was a U.S. Senator, Jack knew it was time to settle down. There was really only one woman Jack could imagine asking to be his wife. So the cat and mouse game he'd been playing with Jackie was about to become a serious courtship.

Chapter 7

LOVE AND MARRIAGE

From the beginning of their romance, Jackie was wary of her feelings for John Kennedy. More than his enjoyment of women, more than his almost reckless pursuit of excitement and pleasure, more than his lack of romantic gestures, Jackie worried that in marrying into the Kennedy family she would somehow lose herself. But she also felt he was a kindred spirit, someone who would be worth the heartache he would inevitably cause her. While it may not have been a match made in heaven, it was one that seemed fated.

Most Eligible Bachelor

Long before Jackie began dating John Kennedy, he had a reputation as a ladies' man. Some friends believed his live-for-today attitude stemmed from having had several brushes with death. His childhood had been full of mysterious illnesses, and he was diagnosed with Addison's disease, a chronic affliction of the immune system, in 1947. His health was complicated by his back injury. Despite being in chronic pain, Washington, D.C.'s most eligible bachelor never seemed to want for female companionship. Although most of his relationships were casual, Jack had been involved seriously, at least by his standards, prior to Jackie.

In 1944, Kennedy met Florence Pritchett, a divorcée who worked as a fashion editor. They became very close, but because she was divorced any talk of marriage to the Catholic Kennedy was out of the question. But Florence was one of the closest relationships Jack ever had—and his physical relationship with her endured well into his marriage and presidency. He would sneak away from his Secret Service detail and rendezvous with Florence at her Palm Beach home. One time the agents assigned to protect him became so distraught at not being able to find him, they called the FBI. Eventually, the Palm Beach police chief, who was a close friend of the Kennedys, directed them to Flo's swimming pool.

During his campaign for the Senate, he dated a woman named Ann McDermott at the same time he and Jackie were going out. For a while, McDermott considered moving to Washington to work in government and to be closer to Jack. But it soon became apparent to her that Jack was not going to be a long-term relationship.

Throughout the time he dated Jackie, Kennedy continued seeing other women, and he never tried to hide his succession of temporary companions and liaisons from his friends and associates. But everyone agreed that he treated Jackie differently than he did the others. Specifically, he wasn't just interested in Jackie as a sex partner. In fact, according to Kennedy's friend Laura Berquist Knebel, Jack never suggested they spend a weekend, or even a night, together. The truth was, while John Kennedy wanted children and a family, he never wanted to get married. But knowing he had to, Jackie was the only woman he could imagine walking down the aisle with.

Courtship

For a while, Jack and Jackie circled each other like prizefighters sizing up their opponents. Both seemed reluctant to be the first one to lay their interest—or heart—on the line. For a while they played it coy. When one started showing more interest, the other would be busy.

Dating a Senator

Eventually, their dating became more regular. Although Jackie did not enjoy attending social functions, she gave in and accompanied the dashing young senator to several. But most of their dates were far more domestic. They often stayed in playing board games like checkers or Monopoly with other friends. Their most private time, when they were alone, was during the car trip back to Merrywood from Washington, D.C., after a date. Jackie thought they shared a similar reserve and once equated their personalities to an iceberg—with most of their emotions hidden below the surface.

Jackie walks along the beach with Jack Kennedy, 1953

Photo Credit: Hy Peskin/Time & Life Pictures/Getty Images

❝❝ SHE SAID . . .

"Jack was something special and I know he saw something special in me, too. I remember my mother used to bring around all these beaus for me but he was different. . . . Both of us knew it was serious, I think, but we didn't talk about it then."

Over the Fourth of July holiday in 1952, Jackie spent the weekend with Jack in Hyannis Port. This was no relaxing holiday getaway. There were raucous games of touch football on the sprawling lawn, tennis, and reminiscences about past games and races. Eunice told Jackie how their parents had trained them in athletics and instilled the importance of winning. Jackie initially felt like a fish out of water. She silently dubbed Jack's sisters the rah-rah girls, and they, in turn, considered her standoffish and snobby. Jackie was appalled at the family's indifference to the arts, and they looked askance at her apparent physical delicateness.

It was that weekend that Joe had a serious talk with Jack about getting married, reminding him that a wife was an important political asset. He also told his son that marriage didn't have to put a crimp in his enjoyment of other women. Joe and Rose had a tacit agreement where in exchange for unlimited funds and the prestige of being a Kennedy, she turned a blind eye to his marital infidelities. He assumed Jackie would be similarly disposed.

On the day of President Eisenhower's inauguration in January 1953, Jackie spent the day working on her Inquiring Camera Girl column, then accompanied Jack to the inauguration as his date. They continued to see each other through the winter and into spring. Jack finally broached the subject of marriage right before Jackie left to cover Queen Elizabeth II's coronation in London.

Uncertainty

Jackie traveled to England with her friend Aileen Bowdoin and saw the trip as a chance to do what she considered real journalism. She filed stories about the voyage and wrote several more about the coronation and the mood in London. She spent a lot of time browsing bookstores buying gifts for Jack. She admitted to Aileen that they had talked about marriage. Rather than being excited Jackie was pensive. It wasn't that she doubted her feelings for him, nor did she doubt his sincerity. It was more a concern about what their life together would be. Being married to a politician would mean living constantly in the public eye. For someone who kept her deepest thoughts and feelings close to her, the idea of living in the spotlight was unnerving. Jackie also worried about being swallowed up by the Kennedy clan. They were such forceful personalities, and she wondered if she'd be able to hold her own and not lose her individual identity.

SHE SAID . . .

"I had a sort of special dress to wear to dinner. I was more dressed up than his sisters were, and so Jack teased me about it, in an affectionate way, but he said something like, 'Where do you think you're going?' And Rose said, 'Oh, don't be mean to her, dear. She looks lovely.'"

THEY SAID . . .

"I said, 'When [Jack] comes to New York, he calls . . . all the guys to line up the girls. The guy is a hopeless womanizer.' And she just laughed. I think basically Jackie was attracted to Jack . . . because all these flaws were balanced by the fact he had money. There was nobody else pursuing her with that kind of money."

—John "Demi" Gates to Sarah Bradford, *America's Queen*

While Jackie's friends may have been concerned, Jack's family was not surprised that he proposed. Ted Kennedy claimed his brother was smitten with Jackie from their first meeting. He said Jack was fascinated by her intelligence and enjoyed her company and conversation. It wasn't a matter of if, just when.

Jack proposed the night Jackie returned from London. She resigned from the *Washington Times-Herald* the next day. On June 24, 1953, Jacqueline Bouvier's engagement to Senator John F. Kennedy was officially announced. That summer, Jack went to Europe with a college friend named Torbert Macdonald and sailed along the French Riviera, sampling the affections of the local female population.

Becoming the Senator's Wife

From the moment they began discussing the wedding details, the relationship between the Kennedys and Jackie's family was strained. Janet wanted a small, understated ceremony and reception. Joe Kennedy saw the occasion as an important publicity opportunity—and it was soon clear that Joe was very much in charge of the couple's pending nuptials. Joe, not Jack, picked out Jackie's custom-designed engagement ring from Van Cleef and Arpels. The ring had an emerald and diamond setting—each stone nearly three carats in size. No expense would be spared to make this the social wedding of the year.

THEY SAID...

"Now that he was about to marry, the Kennedys . . . perceived Jackie as a threat. This was particularly true of Jack's sisters, who called her The Deb, made fun of her baby-like voice and worked relentlessly to engage her in the family's physical activities, where they knew she could never excel."

—Lem Billings, *Jacqueline Onassis*

The Dress

Noted designer Ann Lowe was commissioned by Janet to make Jackie's wedding dress. Lowe, who was born in Alabama, had worked for many *Social Register* families including the Du Ponts and the Auchinclosses. The gown she designed for Jackie featured a portrait neckline and bouffant skirt that was decorated with mini wax flowers. For the bridesmaids, Lowe designed pink faille silk gowns with matching Tudor caps. Jackie later admitted to friends that she didn't like her wedding dress, which accentuated her flat chest and was not flattering to her figure.

Jackie wore her grandmother's lace veil, which was attached to her hair with a small lace tiara decorated with traditional orange blossoms. Her jewelry was minimal: a single strand of family pearls, a diamond leaf pin (a wedding gift from Jack's parents), and a diamond bracelet Jack gave her the night before the wedding. Her wedding bouquet was white and pink spray orchids and gardenias.

The Wedding Party

The rehearsal dinner was held at Newport's Seaside Clambake Club. Jack's brother Bobby was best man, and Ted Kennedy, Charles Bartlett, Michael Canfield, George Smathers, K. LeMoyne Billings, Torbert Macdonald, Charles Spalding, James Reed, Benjamin Smith, Joseph Gargan, R. Sargent Shriver, Paul B. Fay Jr., and Hugh D. Auchincloss III served as ushers.

Jackie's sister Lee was matron of honor and Nina Auchincloss was maid of honor. The bridesmaids included Nancy Tuckerman, Martha Bartlett, Ethel Skakel Kennedy, Jean Kennedy, Shirley Oakes, Aileen Travers, Sylvia Whitehouse, and Helen Spaulding.

One person glaringly absent from the rehearsal dinner was Jackie's father. Black Jack had made every effort to be ready for her wedding. He had cut back on drinking and been working out every day by running around the Central Park reservoir. Although Black Jack had been at the wedding rehearsal and Janet had acquiesced to let him walk their daughter down the aisle, he was not invited to the rehearsal dinner. That night Janet sent Lee's husband to tell Black Jack he would not be welcome at the reception, which was being held at Hammersmith. He took the news hard. He went to the hotel bar and got drunk. When word of her ex-husband's state got to her, Janet disinvited him from the wedding itself. The official story was that Black Jack had come down with an illness that prevented him from attending the wedding. Hughdie walked Jackie down the aisle instead.

The Wedding

On the morning of September 12, 1953, St. Mary's Church in Newport, Rhode Island, was filled to capacity with 750 guests. The church was decorated with white chrysanthemums and pink gladiolas. Archbishop Richard Cushing presided over the forty-minute ceremony. Tenor soloist Luigi Vena sang *Ave Maria*, and a blessing from Pope Pius XII was read.

Jack and Jackie Kennedy sit together at their wedding reception, 1953

Photo Credit: Lisa Larsen/Time & Life Pictures/Getty Images

When the newlyweds emerged from the church, they were greeted by 3,000 spectators. The wedding party drove to Hammersmith Farm in an escorted motorcade for a reception for 1,200 people. The receiving line took two hours to complete before Jack and Jackie were able to enjoy the party. Meyer Davis and his orchestra provided the music, and the first dance for the newlyweds was "I Married an Angel." After the wedding lunch, Mr. and

Mrs. John Kennedy left Hammersmith and stayed two nights at the Waldorf Astoria in New York before flying to Acapulco, Mexico, for a planned two-week honeymoon. But Jack got antsy after a few days, so they flew to Beverly Hills and spent a week visiting his friends before driving to San Francisco to visit Paul Fay and his wife.

FACT

Any baptized Catholic can receive a papal blessing, called Benediction Papalis. To commemorate the blessing, the recipients are sent a certificate made of parchment with hand-painted calligraphy. Most papal blessings are issued to commemorate first communions, confirmations, conversions, marriage anniversaries, and weddings.

Life in the Public Eye

It didn't take Jackie long to realize that marrying into the Kennedy family meant a loss of privacy. Their engagement was national news, and overnight Jackie went from being a local society girl to a public figure. On the day she and Jack registered for their marriage license, Jackie was stunned to find photographers waiting for them outside the county office. At every turn, Joe used his son's engagement as a photo op or as fodder for a published story. As private an occasion as Jackie might have wanted her wedding to be, Joe Kennedy saw it as nothing less than part of his ongoing campaign to get his son elected president. When Jack and Jackie went sailing in Hyannis Port, they were accompanied by a reporter and photographer from *Life* magazine for a story called "Life Goes Courting with a U.S. Senator."

But nothing prepared Jackie for the frenzy her wedding would cause. Yusha called the crowd outside the church unbelievable. When Jackie arrived, she was upset at all the press there and didn't want her picture taken going into the church. When one photographer stuck his lens in her face, Yusha had to push him out of the way to let Jackie pass.

After the ceremony, when she and Jack exited the church, he nudged her forward to pose for the photographers there for several major newspapers and national wire services. The *New York Times* reported that the crowd outside the church was so huge that Jackie was nearly crushed.

Now that they were married, Jackie was expected to attend various dinners and political get-togethers. There was always press at these functions, so as the marriage wore on and her relationship with Jack grew more strained, Jackie dutifully kept a smiling face for the cameras.

THEY SAID...

"She was quite caught off guard by the number of people watching. As were my father and stepmother. Jackie was stunned, sort of dazed by it. But it was a good taste of what was to come, what she would have to get used to."

—Yusha Auchincloss

Assuming the Housewife Role

Jackie originally believed she could continue working as a writer when she got married. But Jack made it clear that it was more important for her to support his political aspirations and be seen as a senator's wife, not as a journalist. The bigger problem for Jackie was that she was also expected now to be a Kennedy above all else. When she and Jack returned from their honeymoon, the house they planned to rent in Georgetown was not yet available, so they moved into a house at the family's Hyannis Port compound. Jackie felt she was under constant supervision by either Joe or Rose, who ruled their family like monarchs overseeing their kingdom.

Jack spent most of the week in Washington, D.C., so Jackie was left to fend for herself. Although she resented some of Joe's rules, such as his insistence she eat dinner with him and Rose every night, at least she had company. Once she and Jack moved into their

Georgetown home in November, Jackie found herself facing the kind of life she had long been disdainful of: that of the dutiful housewife sublimating her own interests for the betterment of her husband's aspirations.

A Woman's Place

Although there have always been women in the American work force, both professional and blue collar, the "normal" occupation was that of housewife and mother. In the 1950s, a woman's place was in the home. It wasn't just a prevailing attitude; it was curriculum.

SHE SAID . . .

"It's a trade-off. There are positives and negatives to every situation in life. You endure the bad things but you enjoy the good. If the trade-off is too painful, then you just have to remove yourself, or you have to get out of it. But if you truly love someone, well. . . . "

In 1963, activist Betty Friedan wrote *The Feminine Mystique*. In it, she analyzed the 1950s dissatisfaction that formed the foundation of the women's movement. To the outside world, the suburban housewife seemed to have it all. But despite being told they were living the American dream, many women were unhappy and personally unfulfilled.

It wasn't that anything was particularly wrong; women simply wanted more than having their lives informed by their children or marriage. They wanted to define themselves. But they worried that something must be wrong with them, so they kept their feelings hidden from friends, not believing anyone else shared their doubts and unease. If they tried talking to their husbands, they were met with either confusion or anger. So throughout the 1950s, few women talked about this restlessness.

The Reluctant Hostess

It was ironic that Jackie ended up married to a senator; politics bored her. At the time of her marriage, she had never once voted in an election. Her disinterest, combined with her ignorance of politics, made her adjustment to being a Beltway hostess all the more

"SHE SAID . . .

"Jack is such a violently independent person, and I, too, am so independent. . . . I found it rather hard to adjust. . . . I was alone almost every weekend. It was all wrong. Politics was sort of my enemy, and we had no home life whatsoever."

difficult. Her increasingly absentee husband didn't help either. At first, Jack came home every evening. But he soon began spending week. ends in either Massachusetts or on the road networking. He went without Jackie, who stayed behind in Washington. She stoically endured reports of Jack being spotted in New York clubs escorting various women. When he did come home, he was usually accompanied by a posse of advisors or associates, as if their home was still a bachelor pad. While their age difference may not have been a factor in their relationship, Jackie's relative youth as a senator's wife made it difficult for her to make friends.

Marriage had not slowed Jack's pursuit of sexual conquests. If anything, he seemed more intent on amassing as many flings and affairs as possible. More than once Jackie was left alone at a party after Jack disappeared for an extended period of time with another woman. Rather than confront him or threaten to leave, she became more introverted. She started chain-smoking and chronically bit her nails.

When the Going Gets Tough

Like Rose before her, Jackie needed a diversion from her marital dissatisfaction. She turned all her creative energies into redecorating their home. She hoped that by making it into a place Jack was proud of, he'd want to spend more time there. But whereas Jackie favored French antiques, silky fabrics, and pastel colors, Jack's tastes were decidedly pedestrian. Her hard work was met with little enthusiasm. Instead of appreciating Jackie's efforts to make herself more appealing by wearing nice clothes, Jack complained about how much money she was spending.

Bored with being bored and desperate to make a connection with her husband, Jackie tried a new tactic: immersing herself in Jack's interests. She read the *Congressional Record*, went to the Senate to hear his speeches, and enrolled in a history class at Georgetown University's School of Foreign Service. Kennedy's publicity machine got *McCall's* magazine to run an article about Jackie's return to school in its October 1954 issue.

Baby Blues

Having babies was a Kennedy tradition. The house in Hyannis Port was filled with Joe and Rose's grandchildren and Jackie was expected to add to the brood as soon as possible. Her inability to get pregnant within the first couple of years of their marriage added to Jackie's discomfort around the Kennedy clan. One of the primary reasons Jack had gotten married was to start a family. So as the years passed without any children to show for it, he began to resent the lost freedom of his bachelor days. Even though his wife captivated him on an intellectual level, he was addicted to the rush of passion that affairs inflamed.

Risky Surgery

Their efforts to conceive were interrupted by Jack's medical condition. His back pain, caused in part by his left leg being an inch shorter than his right, was exacerbated by his football and war injuries, and complicated by his diagnosis of Addison's disease. By the spring of 1954, he could barely walk. Unless Jack agreed to undergo a risky lumbar fusion surgery, doctors predicted he would spend the rest of his life in a wheelchair. Jack decided he would rather be dead than an invalid and opted for the procedure, which was performed on October 21 in New York. He developed a subsequent infection and was so close to death a priest administered the last rites.

Jack recovered but had to undergo a second operation in February 1955 to graft a bone in his spine. After enduring seven months of excruciating recovery, Jack finally returned to the Senate. For the time being, Jack and Jackie moved into Merrywood. Soon,

Jack was again gone more than he was home. Jackie was alone, suffering from bouts of depression.

Heartbreak

Jackie became pregnant in 1955 but miscarried. She became pregnant again in 1956. She was in her final trimester during the Democratic National Convention, at which Jack narrowly missed out on the vice presidential nomination. Angry and frustrated, Jack left to go sailing on the Mediterranean with his father and brother Ted, over Jackie's objections. She was eight months pregnant.

While Jack was gone, Jackie began hemorrhaging and was rushed to the hospital. She underwent an emergency cesarean section, but the baby, a daughter who would have been named Arabella, was stillborn. Jack could not be reached until three days later. Rather than rush home to be by his wife's side, he called Jackie, then finished out his vacation. Friends said he probably wanted to grieve in solitude. Regardless, when he got back, his relationship with Jackie was more strained than ever.

Jackie blamed herself for being unable to bring a baby to term. What she didn't know, however, was that part of her childbearing problems may have been caused by her husband. Doctors now believe that Jackie suffered from chlamydia, a sexually transmitted bacterial disease.

FACT

Chlamydia is the most frequently reported bacterial sexually transmitted disease in the United States. Currently, 2.8 million Americans are infected every year. It is the most common cause of pelvic inflammatory disease (PID), ectopic pregnancy, and infertility in women. The symptoms can be so mild most people are unaware they are infected.

New Beginnings and Endings

His brush with death sharpened Kennedy's political ambitions and his appetite for women. He was encouraged enough by his rising national profile to start thinking about running for the presidency four years down the road in 1960. Not having children would become more and more of an issue the closer Jack came to announcing his candidacy. In early 1957, when Jackie announced she was again pregnant, the entire Kennedy clan held its collective breath.

That July, Black Jack checked into Lenox Hill Hospital for tests. He gave no indication that he was seriously ill. Jackie came to New York to see him, then left to go spend time with her mother. Black Jack had the reputation of being a bit of a hypochondriac, so checking himself into the hospital did not set off any alarm in his family. But on August 3, Black Jack slipped into a coma and died from liver cancer. Jackie was devastated but kept her grief private. She took charge of his funeral arrangements, and Black Jack Bouvier was buried next to his parents and his brother Bud in East Hampton.

Three and a half months later, on November 27, 1957, Jackie gave birth to a healthy baby girl named Caroline Bouvier Kennedy.

Chapter 8

POLITICAL AMBITIONS

Not long after losing out on the vice presidential nomination in 1956, John F. Kennedy began planning his own run for the White House in 1960. As expected, his father's influence and wealth were integral to his campaign. But quite unexpected was how much of an asset Jackie proved to be.

The Political Landscape of 1960

The 1950s had been a time of rest and renewal, and President Dwight Eisenhower, a World War II hero, was finishing up his eight years in office with solid popularity. The country may have projected a *Father Knows Best* public face, but behind closed doors traditional roles were resented and challenged. If Jack was to win the presidency in the 1960 election, he would have to overcome some major obstacles, including his youth and his religion.

Eisenhower

Nobody embodied 1950s social and political conservatism more than President Dwight David "Ike" Eisenhower, considered one of the most popular presidents in American history. He served two terms, from 1953 to 1961, and led America during a time of post-war economic prosperity. He was also the last president born in the nineteenth century.

Eisenhower rose to the rank of general during World War II, eventually overseeing the invasion of Italy. Although some in the military felt Eisenhower's strategies in Italy had been overly cautious, both Winston Churchill and President Franklin Roosevelt were impressed with Ike's ability to successfully command soldiers from different Allied countries. As a result, he was appointed to oversee the invasion of Europe.

FACT

Now known as D-Day, the Allied invasion of Europe began on June 6, 1944, on the coast of Normandy, France. On the first day, 156,000 soldiers landed along a thirty-mile stretch of beach. Tens of thousands of Allied troops died, but the invasion gave the Allies a valuable foothold on the European mainland, which they used to push the Nazis back.

Less than a year after the Normandy invasion, Germany surrendered. Eisenhower retired in 1948 and was appointed president of Columbia University. Four years later he was recruited to be the

Republican Party presidential candidate. Ike and his running mate, Richard Nixon, easily defeated Adlai Stevenson.

Eisenhower's election in 1953 coincided with a move toward conservatism. Jobs were plentiful and America was booming. Americans wanted the good times to keep rolling, and the prevailing mood was one of political and social conservatism. But with that came paranoia and suspicion against anyone who threatened the status quo. Eisenhower continued President Truman's Cold War policies. He fought against the spread of communism both in the United States and abroad.

McCarthyism

Politicians warned that communism was a direct threat to American democracy. The "Red Menace" frightened people enough that they turned a blind eye when a rabidly anticommunist senator from Wisconsin named Joseph McCarthy trampled civil rights in his quest to ferret out communists.

THEY SAID...

"Today we are engaged in a final, all-out battle between communistic atheism and Christianity. The modern champions of communism have selected this as the time. And, ladies and gentlemen, the chips are down—they are truly down."

—Senator Joseph McCarthy, United States Senate

Ambitious and eager to make a name for himself, McCarthy used America's fear of communism to promote his political goals. His assertions were the basis of ongoing hearings that in the end ruined countless lives and ultimately led to McCarthy's official censure. McCarthy was a Kennedy family friend and fellow Catholic. Jack had supported him in the early days of his anticommunist campaign, and he was slow to publicly oppose McCarthy. He was recuperating from back surgery when McCarthy was censured and did not vote on the resolution or declare his support for it.

Civil Rights

Segregation was prevalent throughout the 1950s. In 1954, the landmark Supreme Court ruling in *Brown v. Board of Education* mandated integration, but segregation remained the rule if not the law in much of the country. The Eisenhower administration pledged it would support federal legislation outlawing lynching and poll taxes. Eisenhower also promised to work toward racial integration in the federal government and the armed forces.

THEY SAID...

"I personally believe if you try to go too far too fast in laws in this delicate field that has involved the emotions of so many Americans, you are making a mistake. I don't believe you can change the hearts of men with laws or decisions."

—President Dwight Eisenhower, in *Abundance and Anxiety: America 1945–1960*

Despite his stated agenda, Eisenhower was not a civil rights advocate, politically speaking. Foreign policy was most important to his administration, and to get his policies passed he needed the support of southern Democrats in Congress—who were mostly white segregationists. Kennedy himself did not have a strong record on civil rights in his congressional career, and gaining support from minorities was a challenge for his campaign.

Religion

Through the end of the 1950s, American religion was dominated by the major Protestant faiths. In the years following World War II, Americans returned to church in great numbers. Parents of the baby boomers—children born between 1946 and 1965—had been profoundly affected by the carnage of the war and turned to religion to find comfort from and meaning in the horrors of genocide and atomic destruction. Families flocked to suburbia en masse to enjoy low crime rates, big lawns, and Sunday services. Religion and family became the focal points for Americans trying to regain their footing.

Although the Constitution guaranteed everyone the freedom of religion, America's Protestant heritage was so deeply entrenched that it was extremely difficult for Catholics and Jews to be accepted in high society or advance too far politically. It would take someone with extreme cunning, tireless ambition, and deep—almost limitless—financial pockets to break through. It would take someone like Joe Kennedy.

On the Campaign Trail

By January 1960, Senator John Kennedy was one of the Democratic Party's brightest young stars. He had spent the previous four years building political alliances and increasing his national profile. When he officially announced his candidacy for president on January 20, he was immediately considered the front-runner for the Democratic nomination. After his announcement, Kennedy embarked on a grueling eleven-month campaign, crisscrossing the country to meet—and charm—the public. He gave speeches and appeared on behalf of other politicians. He was the first presidential candidate to effectively use television to promote his message, his candidacy, and, most importantly, his image.

Money Matters

Before the 1960 presidential race, the nominees' campaigns were financed by their respective parties. But because of the ties to corporate America that the Republicans had, their party tended to have more money to spend than the Democrats did. It was believed the disparity in available finances had resulted in several Democratic losses. Kennedy knew firsthand how important money was to a campaign—his father's financial support had been integral to both Jack's congressional and senatorial victories. So Kennedy intended to finance his presidential campaign beyond the scope of the traditional way it had always been. It was reported that Joe

Kennedy had spent more than $1 million before John had even announced his candidacy.

> **FACT**
>
> The cost of campaigning for president—including primary election, general election, and political conventions—has risen sharply since 1960. In January 2007, the chairman of the Federal Election Commission estimated that candidates needed a minimum of $100 million to have a serious chance of winning their party's nomination. Future presidential races are projected to cost in excess of $1 billion.

Kennedy spent money on making his campaign as efficient as possible. In addition to the usual assortment of political advisors and consultants on his campaign staff, he also assembled a specialized campaign staff that included lawyers, accountants, and communications specialists. Although accumulating such a team is now a standard practice, it was revolutionary for its time. Kennedy set up a campaign headquarters near Capitol Hill. Members of his staff then methodically contacted and courted Democrats all over the country, including potential convention delegates.

Primaries

Kennedy's challengers included Senators Hubert Humphrey (Minnesota), Wayne Morse (Oregon), Lyndon Johnson (Texas), and Stuart Symington (Missouri). Jack's strong showing in the primaries effectively knocked Humphrey and Morse out of the race. Winning in a diverse range of states proved that Kennedy appealed to a broad spectrum of voters.

As the national convention approached, it had become a two-man race between Jack and Lyndon Johnson, who did not participate in any of the primaries and declared his candidacy six days before the Democratic convention. Grassroots support for the 1952 and 1956 nominee, Adlai Stevenson, complicated matters, but on July 13, 1960, John Kennedy was named the Democratic candidate for president. In a controversial move that upset liberal supporters—including his brother Bobby—Kennedy selected Johnson as his running mate. But Joe and Jack were pragmatic—Kennedy needed to carry the South to win and Johnson would help him do that. Now the real campaigning began.

A Political Asset

From the beginning of their marriage, Jackie was involved with Jack's political life. She answered mail sent from his constituents, researched articles for him to read, and helped craft some speeches. During his 1958 re-election campaign for the Senate, she had made brief speeches to ethnic groups in their native French, Italian, and Spanish.

Jackie campaigns for her husband before the 1958 election

Photo Credit: Carl Mydans/Time & Life Pictures/Getty Images

The Early Presidential Campaign

Ironically, despite Jackie's involvement in his senatorial campaign, Jack had almost kept Jackie under wraps during his run for the Democratic presidential nomination. He initially expressed reservations about having Jackie play a visible role in his national campaign, worried that many voters may be put off by a cultured, sophisticated, educated wife. He bluntly told Jackie he thought she came across as too aristocratic for the average voter's liking and felt Americans were not ready for someone like her.

His opinion hurt Jackie's feelings, but she remained the dutiful politician's wife. She continued to grant interviews and work behind the scenes. But Joe Kennedy saw Jackie's appeal and urged his son to exploit her potential impact. It didn't take Jack long to realize his father was right, and Jackie became an increasingly visible participant in his campaign.

In early 1960, Jackie accompanied Jack at stops all over the country as he campaigned for president. Kennedy often remarked that Jackie seemed to draw more crowds than he did. Prior to the Wisconsin primary, she filled in for Jack when he had to fly back to Washington for a Senate vote. She traveled through many small towns, explaining her husband's vision and goals for the country. In Kenosha, she commandeered a grocery store's loudspeaker. She stayed consistently on point and never resorted to making any negative comments about Jack's opponent. In a heavily Polish-American community, Jackie charmed the crowd by speaking a little Polish.

Jackie spent three weeks in April and May tub-thumping in West Virginia, commenting that the only way to see her husband was to go campaigning with him. They visited

SHE SAID . . .

"You get so tired you catch yourself laughing and crying at the same time. But you pace yourself and get through it. You just look at it as something you have to do. You knew it would come, and you knew it was worth it. The places blur after a while, they really do."

some of the state's poorest areas, where Jackie was appalled at the poverty and unhealthy living conditions. She sat in shacks talking to the wives of miners and listened to the grievances of striking railroad workers. She told friends that the struggling families she met in West Virginia touched her deeply.

While Jackie enjoyed meeting people as she went from city to city, she found attending fundraisers and political cocktail parties drudgery. Although she told friends she didn't want to be present when political matters were being discussed, behind the scenes, she was a sounding board for Jack.

By the time Jackie discovered she was pregnant in the spring of 1960, she had proven herself a vital, integral asset. Because of her history of miscarrying and Arabella's stillbirth, Jackie was under doctor's orders not to travel. She retreated to Hyannis Port and stayed out of the public eye.

Jackie paints with watercolors while Caroline paints a picture in the background, 1960

Photo Credit: Alfred Eisenstaedt/Time & Life Pictures/Getty Images

Although she couldn't continue the physically arduous traveling necessary for campaigning, Jackie found other ways to still contribute. With the blessing of the Democratic National Committee, she wrote a syndicated column called "Campaign Wife." The idea was for her to discuss issues important to women voters. In all, she wrote six columns from the end of September to right before Election Day. Each column interwove personal stories with Democratic Party policy, focusing on education and health care for the elderly.

THEY SAID...

"When we first married, my wife didn't think her role in my career would be particularly important . . . she felt she could make only a limited contribution. Now, quite obviously, I'm in a very intense struggle—the outcome uncertain—and she plays a considerable role in it. What she does, or does not do, really affects that struggle."

—John F. Kennedy, in *Redbook*

Although she largely disappeared from the public eye in the summer of 1960, she made occasional important appearances. She and Jack were interviewed on the CBS series *Person to Person*. Jackie was also recruited to tape radio commercials for foreign countries, speaking in their native tongue. In addition, she hosted fund-raising teas, sponsored a telephone poll on women's reactions to the presidential campaign, and organized viewing parties for the televised debates between Jack and the Republican candidate, Richard Nixon.

In October, when she was seven months pregnant, Jackie went to New York with Jack and participated in a parade. More than one million spectators lined the route. On several occasions, people broke through the safety barricades and rushed the car, trying to get close enough for an autograph or to just shake the couple's hands. The response somewhat frightened Jackie and may have been the first inkling of the Jackie-mania that was to follow.

> **THEY SAID...**
>
> "I don't think [Kennedy] had any kind of passionate moral vision about politics. John Kennedy was cool. I would say that yes, Jacqueline would certainly have been the source of moral warmth on these issues. . . . He was rationally and morally offended when he learned about the mistreatment of blacks but it was a detached reason that generated him to action."
>
> —Harris Wofford, Kennedy advisor

The Nixons

Early in the campaign, Kennedy's opponents realized that Jackie was the Democrats' secret weapon. There were snide comments about her aristocratic background, which she usually shrugged off with humor. But the observation that Jackie and Pat Nixon were personal and political polar opposites reflected the cultural transformation of women in America. In the media, Pat Nixon represented the pre–World War II mindset of the stay-at-home housewife; Jackie, even though she had given up her writing career, was still the embodiment of the modern post–World War II woman who walked beside her husband in the spotlight, not behind him in the shadows. The irony in that perception is that prior to her marriage Pat Nixon had held down more jobs than possibly any other First Lady.

The Cloth Coat Republican

Pat Nixon was born Thelma Catherine Ryan on March 16, 1912, in Ely, Nevada, where her father worked as a miner. He gave her the nickname Pat because she was born on the eve of St. Patrick's Day. When she was two years old, her family moved to Southern California, where they ran a farm. Pat's mother died of cancer when she was twelve years old. Her father died five years later of silicosis, a lung disease caused by working in a mine.

Pat supported herself through Fullerton Junior College and the University of Southern California by working as a driver, an

❝❝ SHE SAID . . .

"You do what your husband wants you to do. My life revolves around my husband. His life is my life. . . .

I want to take such good care of my husband that, whatever he is doing, he can do better because he has me. His work is so important. And so exciting."

X-ray technician, a cleaner, a department store sales clerk, a typist, and a movie extra. After graduating cum laude with a degree in merchandising, Pat went to work as a teacher in Whittier, California. Pursuing her enjoyment of performing, she joined a theater group and met a young lawyer named Richard Nixon when they were cast together in a play. He proposed on their first date, and they were married three years later in 1940. The Nixons had two daughters, Patricia and Julie.

As Richard Nixon's political career advanced, Pat was portrayed as a devoted model mother and wife who personally ironed her husband's suits. She was named Outstanding Homemaker of the Year in 1953, Mother of the Year in 1955, and Nation's Ideal Housewife of 1957. While her dedication to family earned her admiration, it also earned her the reputation of being a bit drab. Her husband underscored her image in his "Checkers speech" when he commented that Pat didn't own any extravagant furs—just a respectable Republican cloth coat.

QUESTION

What was the "Checkers speech"?

In 1952, Richard Nixon was Eisenhower's running mate. Nixon appeared on national television to deny receiving $18,000 in illegal campaign contributions. He claimed the money was reimbursement for expenses. After a detailed account of their frugal finances, Nixon admitted accepting one gift—a dog named Checkers, which he defiantly announced his kids were going to keep.

Campaign Wife

Not to be outdone by Jackie's high profile, the Nixon camp created an ad campaign, "Pat for First Lady" that was aimed directly at housewives, who they hoped would identify with Pat. Pat Nixon herself urged women to get involved in the political process by volunteering. The national press frequently compared the two candidates' wives, creating a kind of mini-race between the two that focused on their vastly different personal styles.

Individually, Jackie brought a new dimension to politics. Together, she and Jack changed the way the public at large viewed politicians. They had the unique ability to be both accessible and regal. They greeted the common man and the patrician with the same attention and interest, all the while keeping a subtle distance. To many Americans they were a new breed of celebrity—political royalty who symbolized youth, vitality, and class.

A New President and a New Son

Both John F. Kennedy and Richard Nixon campaigned in earnest throughout the late summer and fall. Nixon was considered the front-runner in the presidential race. He was older, was the sitting vice president, and he was perceived as having more experience—despite the fact that he and Jack had served their freshman terms in Congress the same year. Two decisions would prove to be key for Kennedy to win votes.

Confronting the Catholic Issue

Both media reports and his own campaign researchers told him the American public was still suspicious about accepting a Catholic as president. Kennedy knew the only way to calm the suspicions was to confront them, so he accepted an invitation from the Greater Houston Ministerial Association to speak on September 12, 1960.

In his televised speech, he made it clear that his Catholic faith would in no way compromise his position as president if he were to be elected. He expressed his understanding of the suspicions surrounding him but assured the public he also understood the difference between his individual faith and his duties as president of a secular nation.

THEY SAID...

"I am the Democratic Party's candidate for President who happens also to be a Catholic. I do not speak for my church on public matters—and the church does not speak for me. . . . [I]f the time should ever come . . . when my office would require me to either violate my conscience or violate the national interest, then I would resign the office."

—John F. Kennedy

The speech was well received. Kennedy had not shied away from the religious issue; instead, he had gone before a hostile audience to plead his case. The religious issue did not disappear completely, but Kennedy succeeded in diminishing its importance and its impact on his candidacy.

Televised Debates

Kennedy had successfully deflected skepticism about his faith, but he still faced an able opponent in Richard Nixon. Television network executives proposed a series of debates—the first ever televised debates between presidential candidates—and Kennedy jumped at the opportunity. Nixon had greater name recognition than Kennedy, and Kennedy needed a way to establish a level playing field. In contrast, Nixon had nothing to gain and everything to lose from appearing in the debates. Against the warnings of his advisors and President Eisenhower, Nixon readily agreed to the debates, his ego trumping smart political strategy.

Prior to the first debate, Jack prepared by meeting with the debate's producer to discuss camera placement and the design of the set. Nixon insisted on preparing in solitude. An estimated 70 million Americans, representing approximately two-thirds of the electorate, watched the first debate, which was held on September 26,

1960. Kennedy wore a blue suit and blue shirt so he would stand out against the gray background. Nixon wore a gray suit and seemed to blend into his surroundings. Kennedy spoke directly and confidently to the cameras. Nixon directed his responses toward Kennedy rather than to the home audience, a mistake that made him seem disingenuous. Kennedy appeared groomed and handsome. With his five o'clock shadow, Nixon came across as shifty. Three-fourths of the viewers who decided on their vote after that night chose Kennedy.

FACT

In 1950, only 11 percent of American homes had a television set. At that time there were less than fifty stations in the country, mostly located on the two coasts. After the FCC started awarding broadcasting licenses, the industry exploded. By 1960, 88 percent of American homes had televisions.

Election Day

On Election Day, Jackie met Jack in Boston and cast her vote. She later said she only voted for president and no other race because how often could anyone say her husband was on the ballot for president. From there, the couple went to Hyannis Port to wait out the results. The election was one of the closest in history, and both Jack and Jackie went to bed without knowing who had won. When the Secret Service showed up at the Kennedy compound the next day, the family knew Jack was the new president. When Jack walked into Bobby's house, everyone stood. No longer was he their brother, Jack. He was the president, and he would become known as JFK by the public.

While the rest of the Kennedys celebrated, Jackie went for a walk on the beach by herself. Instead of elation, her reaction was thoughtful reflection. She knew her life, her marriage, and her family, would be forever changed. She and Jack were about to become the most public of couples, and every aspect of their lives would come under scrutiny.

John Jr.

In the evening of November 24, Jack left Washington, D.C., for Florida. Jackie was reading Caroline a goodnight story when her labor started. She was rushed to Georgetown University Hospital by ambulance. Within minutes, the entire Washington press corps was alerted that the soon-to-be First Lady was in labor. Efforts to reach Jack on the plane were unsuccessful. When he landed in Florida, he was contacted by the obstetrician, who was about to perform a casarean section. Kennedy—and the reporters traveling with him—took the next plane back to Washington. In the early morning hours of November 25, Jackie gave birth to John Fitzgerald Kennedy Jr. He was the first baby ever born to a president-elect.

In the ensuing weeks, no detail about the soon-to-be First Family was too small. Their every movement was dutifully reported. John Jr.'s baptism was front page news in the *New York Times*. It was the beginning of a national obsession that would both frustrate Jackie and make her the most famous First Lady in White House history.

Chapter 9

A NEW KIND OF
WHITE HOUSE

The White House has always been a symbol of the sitting American president. But prior to the Kennedy presidency, it was seldom seen as a historical monument in its own right. Jackie changed that, transforming the White House into a living historical residence. She oversaw a much-needed makeover that gave the White House a look befitting a public treasure.

America's Power Couple

While President Kennedy radiated youthful vigor and charismatic vitality, Jackie was the embodiment of cool elegance. After Jack's election, they became America's ultimate power couple. But behind closed doors, Jackie struggled to regain her health and emotional bearings before donning her latest role: First Lady.

Transition

Jackie spent two weeks in the hospital after John Jr.'s birth. Although she was still weak, she met outgoing First Lady Mamie Eisenhower for a two-hour tour of the White House. Mrs. Eisenhower, who had assumed she would be passing the White House on to her close friend Pat Nixon, was polite but reserved. Told of Jackie's fragile health, Mamie refused to offer the use of a wheelchair, even though there was one in a nearby closet, unless she was asked. Jackie toughed it out, later admitting she was too embarrassed to ask. The exertion and bitter cold of the wintry day left her exhausted and disgruntled.

After posing for pictures with Mamie Eisenhower, Jackie left with Jack and a team of advisors for the Kennedy Palm Beach compound. She spent her time in Florida organizing the plans for the White House move and jotting down ideas on how to give the imposing mansion a makeover. She also read several design books, and by the time of the inauguration, Jackie had a concrete vision of what the Kennedy White House would be.

Inauguration

January 20, 1961, was sunny but bitterly cold. Jackie and Jack had breakfast together in their Georgetown house. They dressed for the ceremony, then went to meet the Eisenhowers at the White House. The oldest president was about to turn the presidency over to the youngest man ever elected to fill the position. The two men had grown to respect one another over the course of their transitional meetings. Jackie and Mamie made polite but superficial conversation. When Pat Nixon arrived, there was a palpable tension in the room. Kennedy and Eisenhower drove to the Capitol together in one car, followed by Jackie and Mamie in another. The Nixons traveled separately.

Jack's Catholicism was underscored by Cardinal Cushing's participation in the inauguration. Cushing was a close friend of the Kennedys and made it his personal mission to make the American public accept the idea of a Catholic president. After Cushing's prayer invocation, poet Robert Frost movingly recited "The Gift Outright" from memory. Then John Fitzgerald Kennedy was sworn in as the thirty-fifth president of the United States.

SHE SAID . . .

"Oh, God, it's the worst place in the world. So cold and dreary—a dungeon. . . . It looks like it's been furnished by discount stores. I've never seen anything like it. I can't bear the thought of moving in. I hate it, hate it, hate it!"

For the Kennedys, it was the fulfillment of a decades-old family dream. Sixteen of Jack's relatives crowded the platform where the swearing-in took place. Although the Bouviers, Lees, and Auchinclosses were invited, they were mostly spectators for the inaugural festivities. At a luncheon thrown by Joe Kennedy at the Mayflower Hotel and then at the White House reception for the families, neither the Kennedys nor Jackie interacted very much with the other families.

Jackie spent most of the afternoon in bed, exhausted. She was still recovering from John Jr.'s birth, but she was also emotionally drained. The only relative she spent any time with was her cousin Michael Bouvier, whom she had brought up to her bedroom. After spending the day resting, she and Jack left to attend the five inaugural balls. Jackie was only able to make it through two before returning to the White House and going to sleep by herself in the Queen's bedroom while Jack celebrated until the early hours of the morning.

White House Restoration Project

When Jackie was a teenager, she took a tour of the White House with her mother and sister. Even then, she was disappointed by the way it was furnished and frustrated there was no guidebook available for visitors. Twenty years later, as she and Jack prepared to move in, Jackie discovered just how much the mansion had been neglected and fallen into subtle disrepair. During Harry Truman's administration it had been deemed structurally unsafe and underwent extensive rebuilding. But the interior remained more Howard Johnson than national treasure. Jackie wanted the White House to reflect its importance and history instead of dreary blandness. She was particularly interested in bringing the past alive to children so they would be excited about history and about the nobility of public service.

SHE SAID . . .

"All these people come to see the White House and they see practically nothing that dates back before 1948. Everything in the White House must have a reason for being there. It would be sacrilege merely to 'redecorate' it—a word I hate. It must be restored—and that has nothing to do with decoration. That is a question of scholarship."

The White House Fine Arts Committee

Since its completion in 1800, the White House had undergone multiple renovations and expansions, the most recent during the Truman administration. While the reconstruction made the White House structurally sound and habitable, little thought was put into the interior design of the refurbished rooms. The Eisenhowers, coming from a military background where efficiency and serviceability were more important than style and craftsmanship, kept the furnishing generic with little thought to creating a historical showplace.

In addition, many of the older furnishings that had been taken out of the White House were kept in various storage facilities throughout Washington, D.C. But others had either been taken by previous residents when they left or had been auctioned off to the public. Locating the missing furnishings was Jackie's first priority. Within weeks of the inauguration she announced the formation of the White House Fine Arts Committee. Members included experts in historic preservation and decorative arts. The committee tracked down many items, including furniture and artwork that had been owned by other presidents, and succeeded in getting many donated back to the committee. Jackie personally rummaged through the storage facilities, selecting items worthy of being restored and placed in the White House.

FACT
The Oval Office is the president's formal work area. The first Oval Office was built in 1909 on the south side of the West Wing. In 1934 it was moved to its present location overlooking the Rose Garden. The office features a white marble mantel, the presidential seal in the ceiling, and the U.S. and president's flags.

Making a Difference
The first room Jackie renovated was the Oval Office. She installed a desk that had been given to President Rutherford Hayes by Queen Victoria. The desk had been made from timbers belonging to a one-time British sailing ship. The desk is still part of the Oval

Office furnishings, and a replica was created for the Oval Office exhibit at the Kennedy Library and Museum.

Each room was decorated with a theme based on periods of U.S. history. For example, the Green Room was done in a Federal style, the president's study was decorated in a Victorian style, and the Yellow Oval room in Louis XVI. The fabric used for the furniture was created to match designs from each era. Jackie also asked her friend Rachel "Bunny" Mellon to redesign the Rose Garden so it would be suitable for greeting the public and dignitaries alike. The result was a style and sophistication never before seen in the White House. The mansion was no longer just an official residence but an accredited historic house museum honoring both America's proud history and the Founding Fathers.

Jackie expanded her advocacy for historic preservation to include the White House neighborhood. When she discovered that a row of homes along Lafayette Square, across the street from the White House, were going to be torn down by developers to make way for office buildings, Jackie personally intervened. She commissioned a plan that called for erecting the office buildings behind the historical homes and putting a brick façade on them in order to maintain the Square's historical identity.

First Curator

Within weeks of moving into the White House, Jackie successfully lobbied for the creation of a White House curator position. The curator would be in charge of the preservation and collection of the art, furniture, and decorative items used in the White House. Henry Francis Du Pont, who had been appointed the chairperson of the Fine Arts Committee, suggested a young woman who had recently graduated from the preservation program at Du Pont's Winterthur Museum. Jackie took his advice and in March 1961, Lorraine Waxman Pearce was hired as the first White House Curator. It was her first job out of graduate school.

Pearce, who referred to herself as timid and overeducated, reported directly to Jackie. Her job description was to help refurbish the White House in the authentic furnishings and character of the Founders, in the spirit of Jefferson, Adams, Hamilton, and their successors. Initially, the project seemed overwhelming because there was so little to start from. Because the position was so new, there was no staff and very little budget. Pearce's salary was actually paid by the Smithsonian Institution. It was also personally challenging for Pearce, who had a one-year-old son at home.

> **FACT**
> Winterthur is a 983-acre estate located in Delaware. It is the former home of Henry Francis Du Pont, who moved into a smaller house on the estate and converted the main dwelling into one of the world's foremost museums, featuring furniture and decorative arts made or used in the United States prior to 1860.

After the announcement of the renovation, thousands of letters poured into the White House from people who owned or knew of presidential items. One letter led Pearce to acquire two blue armchairs bought by President Monroe. Jackie was away the day the chairs arrived. When President Kennedy stopped by the curator's office to see if anything new had come in and saw the chairs, he and Pearce decided they would be a perfect gift for Jackie. She was thrilled, both by the chairs and her husband's sentiment.

The White House: An Historic Guide

Although Jackie's agenda was strictly aesthetic, she was aware that everything in Washington had potential political ramifications. As it was, she and Pearce had to convince skeptics that a professional guidebook/catalog was an essential tool in the process of turning the White House into a historical museum. In the planning of the first official White House guidebook, Jackie opted against using public funds to publish it outright. She formed a nonprofit organization called the White House Historical Association to publish the guidebook, which would be offered for sale to all visitors. Profits from the publication would be used to help finance the restoration project and pay for items located by the Fine Arts Committee.

Developing the Guide

Working with Pearce, Jackie assisted in all aspects of the book: She helped select the photographs to illustrate the guide, designed the layout, and approved the text, which Pearce wrote. Jackie's hands-on involvement coupled with her artistic taste and aesthetic vision paid off. Within six months after its 1962 publication, *The White House: An Historic Guide* sold half a million copies. The book is currently in its twenty-second edition and continues to fund the White House Historical Association.

Pearce remained curator for eighteen months before leaving to raise her children. She later established an antiques business and lectured and tutored on the decorative arts out of her Georgetown home, a four-story ship captain's house built in 1810.

Televised Tour

The public response to the renovation was overwhelmingly positive. To let Americans see the progress, Jackie conducted a televised tour of the White House, which CBS broadcast on February 14, 1962.

A record 56 million viewers watched as the First Lady guided the audience through the newly restored rooms. She used the network exposure to explain her belief that the White House was more than a private residence for the sitting president; it should be a showcase for art and culture, a source of national pride, and a place every American should visit. The broadcast was a huge success, and Jackie was later awarded an honorary Emmy for public service.

SHE SAID . . .

"I think if [young students] can come here and see . . . this building and—in a sense—touch the people who have been here, then they'll go home more interested. I think they'll become better Americans. Some of them may want to someday live here themselves—which I think would be very good."

Showcasing the Arts

Jackie's public show of support for the arts began with the inauguration. She convinced Jack to invite artists from all the creative fields to the ceremony. Their presence was a visual symbol of the new administration's celebration of artistic achievement and heritage. At White House dinners, politicians and dignitaries mingled with actors, musicians, artists, and literary figures. In the East Room, Jackie had a portable stage built for live performances, including a series of concerts for young people. She also hosted performances of opera, ballet, Shakespeare, and modern jazz. It was also her vision to build a national cultural complex in Washington, D.C.—an idea that eventually became the Kennedy Center for the Performing Arts.

Jackie with the cast of the American Ballet Theatre's production of *Billy the Kid* at a dinner for the president of the Ivory Coast, 1962

Her efforts were not limited to preservation of U.S. history. When ancient temples were threatened by floods caused by the construction of the Aswan Dam in Egypt, Jackie became involved in saving them.

Dining at the White House

Jackie's familiarity with Europe, her love of other cultures, and her fluency in French and Spanish made her America's most popular unofficial ambassador. When foreign dignitaries came to the United States, Jackie charmed them with her intelligence and style. Rather than just hosting a traditional protocol-heavy dinner, Jackie elevated presidential entertaining into occasions imbued with culture. She personally choreographed every detail of state dinners so they would project the Kennedy image of vitality and sophistication.

FACT

Under United States protocol rules, a state dinner is a formal dinner held for a foreign head of state, such as a king or president. An official dinner is held in honor of a head of government, such as a prime minister. Other foreign dignitaries, such as Britain's Prince Charles, are feted with a social dinner.

Traditionally, dinner guests were seated in tables configured to look like a giant horseshoe or an E. Jackie preferred seating people at round tables set for either eight or ten, which was more conducive to conversation. The linen tablecloths were embroidered and the glassware came from West Virginia. French chef René Verdon prepared the menus. After the meal, guests were treated to live performances. It seemed everything Jackie touched turned to presidential gold. It didn't take long for the Kennedy style of entertaining to make their dinners the most sought-after invitation in Washington.

FACT

Jacques Pépin, the noted French chef and former chef to Charles de Gaulle, turned down the opportunity to serve as President Kennedy's chef at the White House. Instead, Pépin accepted a position in the test kitchen at Howard Johnson's. He went on to become a successful cookbook author and television personality.

There were two dinners in particular that had significant historical importance. On November 13, 1961, the Kennedys hosted a dinner for Puerto Rican governor Luis Muñoz Marin and his wife. Pablo Casals, the legendary Spanish cellist, performed that night. In 1904 Casals had played for President Theodore Roosevelt but had sworn he would never perform in America again after the U.S. government recognized Generalissimo Franco's fascist regime in Spain. While he declined the invitation to dinner, Casals agreed to perform after President Kennedy's personal request. In the audience to hear Casals were some of the most noted American composers and conductors, including Leonard Bernstein, Aaron Copland, and Samuel Barber.

THEY SAID...

"Washington is striving to erase a long-held notion—that, compared to other world capitals, it's a cultural hick town where there's nothing to do at night. The White House has set a new tone in making it an agreeable and fashionable civic duty to encourage the arts."

—January 1962 issue of *Look* magazine

On April 29, 1962, the Kennedys hosted a dinner honoring forty-nine of America's most distinguished educators, scientists, and artists, including several Nobel laureates. The guest list included Pearl S. Buck, Robert Frost, James Baldwin, Linus Pauling, Robert

Oppenheimer, and John H. Glenn Jr. The assembled group was so distinguished that Jack called it "the most extraordinary collection of talent, of human knowledge, that has ever been gathered together at the White House—with the possible exception of when Thomas Jefferson dined alone."

Chapter 10

BEFORE THE STORM: AMERICA OF THE EARLY 1960S

The early 1960s seemed to be a time of endless possibilities. America's young president energized the country—and challenged it. Kennedy urged his fellow countrymen to be proactive citizens rather than passive observers. He encouraged them to make the country a better place through individual commitment to higher ideals and goals. While the man himself may have been a less than stellar role model and husband, what he and Jackie symbolized to the public was the untapped potential of the country.

A Country in Transition

On the surface, the first years of the 1960s were not noticeably different from the 1950s. The majority of Americans were content to be swept along by their young president's enthusiastic exhortations of possibility. But looking deeper, a number of social fissures were deepening. Dissent over issues such as civil rights, equality for women, gay rights, and concern over the conflict in Southeast Asia was still polite but becoming more vocal—especially among younger Americans. While their parents may have grown up being told children should be seen and not heard, the youth of the 1960s believed they had a right to free expression, one they would use it in an unprecedented way.

FACT

Baby boomer is a term used to describe people born between 1946 and 1965. The boom occurred in many countries following World War II. In America, live births went from 222,721 in January 1946 to 339,499 that October. By the end of the boom, four out of ten Americans were under the age of twenty.

The sixties were the age of youth, as 70 million children born in the years following World War II became teenagers and young adults. Rather than accept the status quo, they felt empowered to make a change and to leave their mark on the United States and the world. As baby boomers came of age, they questioned social attitudes their parents had accepted. Boomers had grown up in relative prosperity. The boomers were the generation of change and experimentation, both artistically and socially. Often, artists led the way in clamoring for social change or facilitated change by their very existence. Bob Dylan, the Beatles, Jimi Hendrix, Motown, and artists like Andy Warhol and Roy Lichtenstein made pop art a respectable genre.

The Kennedy White House was a bridge between the old and the new. While still holding on to many of the traditional social roles of previous generations, Jack and Jackie also exuded an individual sense of style. That individuality struck a chord with America's youth. The changes the early boomers set in motion would eventually change the very fabric of American culture. The effort to change society for the better, to make it more inclusive and more responsible to all citizens continues to this day.

> **FACT**
> The first oral contraceptive pill was approved for use in America in 1960. The availability of reliable contraception had an enormous impact on society in general and women in particular. Controlling pregnancy allowed women to be more sexually adventurous. The Pill also allowed couples to better manage the number of children they had; consequently the average size of American families decreased.

The cultural revolution was not confined to America. Countries all over the world experienced a rush of social changes. During the 1960s the British colonial empire was essentially completely dismantled; in Africa, new-found freedom frequently led to civil war; minorities the world over demanded equality. The sixties became synonymous with change, upheaval, subversiveness, independence, and passion over causes that would both unite and divide the country.

The Cold War

President Kennedy's foreign policy was based on the politics of the Cold War, the standoff between the communist Soviet Union and its allies and the democratic United States and its allies that began shortly after World War II. Under President Truman, the United States embraced a policy of containment. The United States opposed new communist regimes in an effort to limit the spread of communism beyond China, the Soviet Union, and its sphere of influence in Eastern Europe. The United States feared that if left unchecked, communism would spread throughout the world and threaten democracy.

As a senator, Kennedy had supported containment and had taken a tough stance against communism. During his presidency, the two superpowers would come to the brink of nuclear war over the Cuban missile crisis. But they would also take an unprecedented step toward peace with the Nuclear Test Ban Treaty.

The Great Divide

By 1961, the Soviet-implemented communist system in East Berlin was withering. From 1949 to 1961, more than 2.6 million East Germans escaped from their bleak circumstances into West Berlin. They represented 15 percent of the country's entire population. The East German leader, Walter Ulbricht, devised a plan that literally walled off East Berlin from West Berlin.

FACT

The border between East and West Berlin and the two Germanys was more than one hundred miles long. It was manned by 25,000 armed guards with orders to shoot to kill. Over the twenty-eight years of the wall's existence, more than 100 people were shot trying to reach freedom.

Ulbricht called his plan the "Wall of China." The first step was to close all the crossing points. A military zone was then established along the border. The subway was halted, and roadways that ran between the two cities were destroyed. Stone barricades were set up and tanks blocked the checkpoints. In August 1961, construction crews began to build a permanent wall. To Americans watching from abroad, it was a sign that their deep mistrust and fear of the Soviets were justified.

On June 26, 1963, President Kennedy visited West Berlin. He gave a speech criticizing communism and extolling the human spirit of those trapped behind the wall. Some of the countries under

Soviet rule tried, unsuccessfully, to exert that human spirit and claim their independence during the Cold War. In 1956 Hungary's leader, Imre Nagy, sought to implement social reforms and free election. He was removed from office and executed. A dozen years later, Czechoslovakia's Alexander Dubcek tried to establish a liberal form of socialism that gave citizens more personal freedoms. Called the Prague Spring, censorship was lifted and free expression encouraged. But it came to an abrupt end on August 20, 1968, when Soviet tanks rumbled through the streets of Prague, as they had in Budapest. Dubcek was arrested and forced to publicly swear loyalty to Soviet communism.

The Vietnam War

President Eisenhower supported South Vietnam's struggle against communist North Vietnam, but during Kennedy's presidency it looked as though the South Vietnamese might be defeated. Kennedy stepped up U.S. involvement in Vietnam.

In an effort to stop the spread of communism in Southeast Asia, President Kennedy sent 16,000 U.S. Special Forces and advisors to Vietnam to support the South Vietnamese government, led by Ngo Dinh Diem. But the South Vietnamese Army was losing ground to the North Vietnam-supported Viet Cong. Worried that Diem might compromise with the rebels and install a government that included communist delegates, Kennedy agreed that Diem should be removed from office. He was deposed in a coup d'état in November 1963 and was killed the next day. The U.S. military did not participate in the coup but did not defend Diem either.

FACT

Officially, 58,148 Americans were killed during service in the Vietnam War. An additional 114 were captured and died in captivity. It is estimated that 9,000 veterans committed suicide as a direct result of the war. The total number of Vietnamese killed, North and South, military and civilian, was approximately 5.4 million.

There is compelling evidence that Kennedy was planning on pulling out of Vietnam after the 1964 presidential election—a move vice president Lyndon Johnson strongly disagreed with. On October 11, 1963, Kennedy ordered the withdrawal of 1,000 military personnel from Vietnam by the end of 1963. But once Lyndon Johnson became president, that order was reversed and the war escalated. The first protests against the war began in 1963, but the antiwar movement did not organize in earnest until 1965 after President Johnson began bombing North Vietnam and sent in a surge of U.S. troops.

Space Race

The space race between the United States and the Soviet Union began in 1957 when the Russians were the first to launch an artificial satellite, *Sputnik*. The achievement gave Russia bragging rights to claim the achievement and showed their technology was superior to America's.

QUESTION

What was the first living being in space?

In November 1957, the Soviets launched *Sputnik 2*. On board was a dog named Laika, who became the first living creature to go into orbit. A few hours into orbit, Laika died from apparent stress and overheating. In 1961, Khrushchev presented the Kennedys with a dog named Pushinka, a daughter of one of the first dogs to successfully return to earth after being shot into orbit.

Not only was conquering space an important scientific victory, it also had military implications. Americans were already nervous about the Soviets' perceived military might, especially the potential development of intercontinental ballistic missiles. The idea that the Soviets were ahead of America in the space race added to the anxiety. But President Eisenhower did not show much interest in either space programs or cosmic exploration. President Kennedy, however, did.

A turning point came on April 12, 1961 when a twenty-seven-year-old Soviet fighter pilot named Yuri Gagarin was sent into space on the world's first piloted space mission. His spacecraft, *Vostok*, orbited the earth once before re-entering the atmosphere and bringing Gagarin safely back to land. It was an electrifying event and put the Soviets clearly ahead in the space race.

Gagarin's flight had a profound effect on Kennedy. He took it as a personal affront against America's honor. On May 5, 1961, a former navy test pilot named Alan Shepard became the first American in space with a fifteen-minute flight. Americans responded with wild enthusiasm, and Kennedy saw an opportunity to both regain the lead in the space race and to unite Americans in a common cause. Less than a month after Shepard's flight, Kennedy made a stunning announcement to Congress: America should work to put a man on the moon. Although many members of Congress thought the idea was science fiction, the National Aeronautics and Space Administration (NASA) rose to the challenge and began crafting a plan to achieve the goal of a lunar landing.

Over the next several years, the United States launched numerous manned flights, but the Soviets always remained one step ahead. What Americans didn't know then was that many of these achievements were done at extreme risk to the Soviet cosmonauts. Soviet premier Nikita Khrushchev was willing to sacrifice cosmonauts if it meant keeping the illusion of superior Russian technology. Kennedy was assassinated before his dream was realized, but his commitment to the program ensured its survival. Eventually, through the Gemini and Apollo missions, the United States caught and surpassed the Soviet space program.

> **THEY SAID...**
>
> "I believe this nation should commit itself to achieving the goal, before this decade is out, of landing a man on the moon and returning him safely to the Earth. . . . No single space project in this period will be more impressive to mankind, or more important for the long-range exploration of space. And none will be so difficult or expensive to accomplish."
>
> —John F. Kennedy

By the beginning of 1968, America and the Soviets were in a dead heat. But by the end, two failed Soviet lunar missions gave the United States the lead in the space race, which it would never relinquish. On July 20, 1969, astronaut Neil Armstrong climbed down the ladder of his lunar craft and walked on the moon. Kennedy's bold challenge had been answered.

The Fight for Civil Rights

Prior to the mid-1950s, the fight for racial equality in America was largely fought in the courts and on the floor of Congress, and there was little change in the daily lives of most Americans. By the early 1960s, the fight for equality had taken to the streets. While the National Association for the Advancement of Colored People (NAACP) continued its fight in the courts, individual activists, grassroots groups, and churches promoted a more direct response by organizing nonviolent protests, boycotts, sit-ins, and marches. Civil disobedience became the cornerstone strategy of the movement's most influential and visible leader.

Dr. Martin Luther King Jr.

Dr. King first came to prominence as president of the Southern Christian Leadership Council (SCLC). During his tenure he directed a campaign of nonviolent civil disobedience. The success of the Montgomery bus strike in 1955–1956 catapulted King into the national spotlight. From there he used other marches, strikes, and rallies to draw national attention to the plight of minorities in America. His passionate speeches played to the sense of fairness and justice, prompting sympathetic whites to join the civil rights cause.

FACT

On December 1, 1955, in Montgomery, Alabama, Rosa Parks refused to give up her seat on the bus for a white rider and was convicted of disorderly conduct. King organized a thirteen-month bus boycott that reduced bus earnings by 60 percent. A federal court ordered Montgomery to desegregate its buses.

Kennedy and Civil Rights

As a senator, John F. Kennedy strove for the political middle ground on civil rights, neither embracing the movement nor disregarding it. During his run for the White House, Kennedy courted the African American vote. He pledged to support civil rights legislation if he was elected, but King remained unconvinced and declined to endorse Kennedy.

Mere weeks before the election, King was arrested for his participation in a sit-in. A judge handed down a harsh sentence of four months of hard labor; he deemed King had violated the terms of his probation for a traffic offense. Coretta Scott King, six months pregnant with the couple's third child, feared for her husband's safety. Kennedy heard of her distress and called her. His compassionate action did not go unnoticed. In addition, Jackie strongly urged Jack to work for King's release, explaining why it was philosophically important for him to do so. Her emphatic position was a factor in Kennedy's eventual intervention, which resulted in King's release. Martin Luther King Sr., who had previously endorsed Nixon, publicly declared his support for Kennedy.

THEY SAID...

"Because this man was willing to wipe the tears from my daughter [-in-law]'s eyes, I've got a suitcase full of votes, and I'm going to take them to Mr. Kennedy and dump them in his lap."

—Martin Luther King Sr.

Martin Luther King Jr. thanked Kennedy for his help but stopped short of endorsing his candidacy. King became even more disillusioned with the Kennedy administration, which he charged did not do enough to advance civil rights. He was unmoved by the political argument that Kennedy lacked the clout to push civil rights legislation through Congress because his margin of victory had been so narrow.

In June 1963, Kennedy introduced civil rights legislation to Congress. King was instrumental in planning a March on Washington for Jobs and Freedom to pressure Congress to pass the civil rights legislation. Despite Kennedy's protests that the march might alienate potential congressional supporters, the event took place in August 1963. The defining moment of the day was Dr. King's moving "I Have a Dream" speech, which he delivered in front of the Lincoln Memorial.

Kennedy was assassinated before Congress approved the civil rights legislation, but President Johnson worked to ensure its passage, and it was approved on July 2, 1964. Dr. King's dedication to civil rights for all people, regardless of color or creed, and his insistence on doing it peacefully, earned him the Nobel Peace Prize in 1964.

Chapter 11

A SENSE OF STYLE

It's ironic that the young woman who was so painfully insecure about her body and appearance would mature into America's most famous fashion trendsetter. What made Jackie's fashion sense so captivating to so many women was that she selected clothes that were both functional and feminine. She was the epitome of style with substance, and she would influence a generation of women.

Jackie's Personal Sense of Style

An interest in fashion ran in Jackie's family. Her father, Black Jack Bouvier, always dressed impeccably, wearing custom-made clothes and a homburg, a felt hat similar to a fedora. He had his Stutz car specially built so that he could get in the back without taking off his hat. While not quite so flamboyant, Jackie inherited her father's appreciation of style. Her taste was also deeply influenced by her time in Europe, where she admired the elegant creations of French designers.

The President and First Lady after the First Anniversary Inaugural Salute Dinner, 1962

Photo Credit: Cecil Stoughton, White House/John F. Kennedy Presidential Library and Museum, Boston

A Glamorous Image

Part of Jackie's appeal as First Lady was her youth. She was young enough to embrace a woman's right to be a working professional if she chose, but her upbringing still held enough influence over her to sublimate her own goals to those of her husband. Her fashion sense reflected the same dichotomy. On one hand, she expressed her individuality by donning a stylish wardrobe that was classic but modern. Although created by an American designer, the clothes paid homage to French fashions with their sleek lines. She managed to appear glamorous and practical at the same time. Jackie's inaugural dress, made from ivory-colored satin, set the tone for her signature look. She would establish a new standard for a generation of women who wanted more glamour in their lives without sacrificing their own identity.

THEY SAID...

"She observed the upper class conventions, but underneath a veil of lovely inconsequence she developed a cool assessment of people and an ironical slant on life. One soon realized that her social graces masked tremendous awareness, an all-seeing eye, ruthless judgment, and a steely purpose. Her response to life was aesthetic rather than intellectual or moralistic."

—Arthur M. Schlesinger

Fashion in Politics

But Jackie was also aware that perception was all-important in politics. Up to the 1960 presidential campaign, Jackie had always favored French designers, such as Givenchy, Chanel, and Christian Dior. But as soon as her husband ran for president, she came under increased scrutiny. The fashion trade paper *Women's Wear Daily* was critical of what it called her Francophile fashion tendencies. Nixon's wife Pat immediately tried to take political advantage by making sure the media knew that she only wore American-made clothes. The controversy bemused Jackie, as did all the media discussions about her hairstyles and the amount of money she spent on clothes. In one of her "Campaign Wife" columns, she wondered what her hair or clothes had to do with her husband's ability to be president.

> **FACT**
>
> Media reports claimed that Jackie spent $50,000 on her wardrobe in the first fifteen months of the Kennedy administration. Jackie scoffed at the stories, commenting that the only way she could spend that much would be to buy sable underwear.

Jackie was never comfortable with being in the eye of the media. But she was acutely aware that she was now part of history and that people the world over would be following her actions. She also realized everything she said, did, or wore would somehow reflect on her husband's administration, so she was determined to make as strong an impression as possible.

Fashion of the Early 1960s

As the decade began, women's fashion was still very much influenced by the conservative mores of the 1950s. Suburban housewives and mothers wore proper dresses that hung modestly to the knee or below. Girdles were still a must-have accessory, as were petticoats. Pants were seldom worn except for outdoor activities. Colors were muted so as not to draw attention to the fashions or the wearer.

Enter 1960

But winds of change were stirring. Designers began experimenting with stronger, bolder colors. For the first time, the country's youth—the first of the baby boomers coming into maturity—began to influence fashion and other social and cultural trends. Bellbottom pants, inspired by navy uniforms, gained popularity. Casual clothing gained a foothold.

By mid-decade, casual attire was more than a comfortable alternative to suits and dresses—it became a political statement, a break from the status quo. Tie-dyed T-shirts boasting an explosion of color were a statement of individuality.

As the women's movement gained momentum, the younger generation expressed its independence by disregarding the modest norms of the 1950s. Instead of hiding their legs beneath prim dresses, they celebrated skin. Miniskirts and minidresses daringly raised hemlines above the knee. As the skirts became shorter, women would often wear colorful tights underneath.

QUESTION

What is tie-dying?

Tie-dying is a form of clothing design. If a piece of clothing is tied with something like string or rubber bands, the dye cannot reach that bound material. The resulting design is swirling patterns of color. While tie-dyed clothing became synonymous with the 1960s hippie movement, it is an ancient art that dates back more than 1,000 years to China and Japan.

New Trends

Although the miniskirt is remembered for its revolutionary impact on women's fashion, another trend developed that would have a more lasting impact. Jeans were popular, but many women wanted nicer pants that could be worn in a more professional capacity. Tailored trousers gained popularity. They were either worn with a tunic, a shirt, or a matching suit jacket.

The development of new fabrics had an important impact on fashion in the 1960s. When natural fibers were blended with synthetics, it improved the wear of the fabrics. By the 1960s the production of synthetic fibers had become a burgeoning global industry for companies like Du Pont and ICI. Fabrics like Dacron, Spandex, and Lycra became household names and were used in everything from bras to swimming suits. Other synthetics such as Dynel and Teklan were used to make faux furs and fake hair for wigs.

But the fashion revolution was still to come when Jackie was thrust in the world spotlight as First Lady. Her decision to add unapologetic elegance was groundbreaking. Although Jackie would have preferred to commission French designers for her official wardrobe, it was politically problematic. So Jackie went in search of an American designer with European sensibilities.

Jackie's Look

In August 1960, Jackie sent a letter to Diana Vreeland. In it she acknowledged that she needed to buy American clothes and make sure it was publicized. Vreeland, a well-known fashion columnist, suggested Jackie check out the designs of U.S. talent such as Stella Sloat, Ben Zuckerman, and Norman Norrell.

Oleg Cassini

The influential social columnist Igor Cassini—who wrote under the pseudonym Cholly Knickerbocker—heard that Jackie was interviewing designers. Igor, who had once named Jackie Debutante of the Year, suggested to his brother Oleg, a moderately successful designer, that he should submit some designs. Oleg was already familiar to the family because he had gotten to know Joseph Kennedy through the New York City social scene. Oleg wrote Jackie prior to the November 8 presidential election pitching himself for the job. She responded by asking him to submit some sketches. She liked what she saw and asked Cassini to start work on her spring wardrobe.

FACT

Oleg Cassini Loiewski was born in Paris on April 11, 1913. He immigrated to the United States in 1936 with $35 in his pocket, a dinner jacket, and a tennis racket. Cassini designed for film, television, and theater and made ready-to-wear clothes for clothing store sales. Working with Jackie made Cassini one of the most well-known designers of the 1960s, and he went on to run his own design empire.

A Distinct Look

Jackie told Cassini she wanted to dress as if her husband were president of France. He reportedly made more than 300 outfits for Jackie, which Joe Kennedy paid for. The wardrobe Oleg conceived was intentionally reminiscent of Givenchy and other French designers. He made the clothes in the bright, solid colors Jackie favored. He added coat pockets and large buttons so the clothes would be more photogenic. Jackie became known for Cassini's simple, geometric dresses featuring sleeveless A-lines, three-quarter length sleeves, overblouse dresses, and mantillas.

> **FACT**
>
> The First Lady's most famous fashion accessory, the pillbox hat, was the creation of a then-unknown milliner named Halston. Jackie wore a pillbox hat at the inauguration and sparked a new trend. The ensuing popularity of the fashion accessory made Halston a household name and helped launch his clothing design career.

Jackie's decision to make Cassini her only designer surprised many in the industry. For one thing, Oleg had been around a long time without ever distinguishing himself as a trendsetter. In addition, he was best known for sexy, body-hugging designs—definitely not the image of a First Lady. But the sketches he submitted fit Jackie perfectly. They were stylish but understated and suggested a sleek elegance. They would make Cassini the most famous designer in the world.

Symbols of Possibility

The public image of the Kennedys was one of enthusiasm, vitality, and opportunity. There was an energy in the country that had been missing during the Eisenhower years. John F. Kennedy challenged Americans to be proactive citizens. Jackie led by example, publicly committing herself to the arts and historic preservation. She also promoted children's causes such as education, welfare, and artistic awareness. While the president and first lady became symbols of what individual Americans could achieve, their life was not as charmed as it appeared to the public.

Solitude

Soon after the inauguration, Jackie made a conscious effort to establish a life for herself and her children that was independent of politics and the White House. She requested a house in the country where she could take Caroline and John. The family leased a house near Middleburg, Virginia, called Glen Ora, about an hour outside of Washington, D.C. On average, she and the children would spend two long weekends a month there. Although Jackie always looked glamorous and energetic during her public appearances, she was frail and vulnerable. Her long recovery from her difficult pregnancy and the stress of moving into the White House combined with the constant media scrutiny took its toll on her physically and emotionally.

FACT

Middleburg, Virginia, was established in 1787 by Levin Powell. He bought the land on which Middleburg was built at a cost of $2.50 an acre from Joseph Chinn, who was George Washington's first cousin. Once called Chinn's Crossroads, Powell renamed the town Middleburg because it was located midway between the two nearest cities on the Ashby Gap trading route.

While she was away, Jackie continued to conduct business via phone calls and courier. But most of her time was spent playing with her children, teaching Caroline to ride, shopping in local stores, and taking walks. Jackie and the children ate most of their dinners quietly at home, and the only people she regularly socialized with were the parents of Caroline's local friends. Jackie loved the countryside so much that at the end of the year, the family bought thirty-nine acres on a secluded hillside. They built a house there and named the property Wexford after the county in Ireland from which Jack's ancestors hailed.

The Kennedy family, 1962

Photo Credit: Cecil Stoughton, White House/John F. Kennedy Presidential Library and Museum, Boston

Self-Sacrifice

While part of Jackie's desire to carve out her own space was to give her children a safe haven, she was also driven to solitude by the ongoing problems in her marriage. Exacerbating the pain of Jack's infidelities was the fact that it was an open secret among the White House press corps. At the time, it was unthinkable to report on the extracurricular sex life of a president, though Jack's womanizing and the tension between him and Jackie was common knowledge.

Prior to being inaugurated, Jack assumed he would have to curb his extramarital affairs. But once he was in office, his womanizing actually intensified. He even had a long on-again, off-again affair with Jackie's press secretary Pam Turnure. Ironically, it was Jackie's graceful demeanor and elegance, along with her fierce loyalty, that provided Jack with his best cover.

THEY SAID...

"Jackie was a realist, and she must have accepted certain problems in their marriage. But remember: JFK admired her, adored her and was enormously proud of her. She loved Jack in spite of all his infidelities and he loved her—in spite of all his infidelities."

—Arthur Schlesinger, special assistant to President Kennedy

Jackie might have presented a united front with her husband publicly, but privately she frequently expressed her pain at Jack's infidelities. Prior to his election, she expressed doubts that she could stay in the marriage. But Jackie knew the consequences of divorce went far beyond the breakup of a family. It would have forever shattered Kennedy's chance to be president. She had a deeply rooted sense of duty, and staying with her husband despite his infidelities was part of that. She did not want to subject her children to divorce the way she had suffered through her parents' breakup. But perhaps there was a larger reason. For all the heartache his philandering caused her, Jackie remained hopelessly enamored with her husband.

The Dark Side of Camelot Revealed

As invasive as Jackie found the tabloids, it was a respected, Pulitzer Prize–winning investigative journalist who aired the dirty marital laundry Jackie had worked so hard to keep private during her life. In 1997, three years after Jackie's death, Seymour Hersh published *The Dark Side of Camelot*, a book he researched for five years. In it, Hersh documents, in painstaking detail, accounts of Jack's affairs and his alleged efforts to assassinate Fidel Castro.

Light Dalliances

According to Hersh, the night before his inauguration, Jack had a rendezvous with a young woman he'd been seeing for four years—ever since she was a nineteen year-old Radcliffe college student—at the Georgetown house where Jackie and the children had been living. In the spring of 1960, Jack became involved with a call girl named Alicia Darr who later tried to extort money from the Kennedys by threatening to go public.

Hersh described how Secret Service agents were frustrated by the women Jack brought into the White House for one-night stands. For obvious reasons, none of them were screened before showing up, so the agents worried for the president's safety. When he was traveling, local officials often arranged for young women to visit the president—occasionally more than one at a time. Some were political groupies or would-be actresses or party girls; some were high-class call girls. When Jackie was away from the White House, Jack would indulge in lunchtime skinny-dipping with two staff aides, known around the White House as Fiddle and Faddle. When Jackie was in residence, Jack refrained from extramarital activities—but the majority of her time was spent away from Washington in Virginia. Whenever Jackie was preparing to return to the White House she called to announce her pending arrival to avoid any awkward confrontations.

Worrisome Affairs

While most of Jack's infidelities were one-time encounters, some developed into ongoing affairs. In 1960 Frank Sinatra introduced Jack to a beautiful twenty-five-year-old California socialite named Judith Campbell. Within the month they began an affair. According to Hersh, Jack later asked Campbell to take a satchel containing a quarter million dollars to Chicago mobster Sam Giancana, who Campbell also knew through Sinatra. The money was for Giancana's help in securing the Illinois vote for Jack. Throughout the presidential primaries Campbell continued to act as a go-between for Giancana and Kennedy. After Kennedy ended the affair, Campbell became Giancana's lover.

❝SHE SAID . . .

"[Bess Truman] brought a daughter to the White House at a most difficult age, and managed to keep her from being spoiled so that she has made a happy marriage with a lovely child of her own. Mrs. Truman kept her family together in spite of White House demands, and that is the hardest thing to do."

Because of her association with Giancana, the FBI had Campbell under surveillance so her affair with Jack soon came to the attention of J. Edgar Hoover. The FBI's top man did not make the affair public, mostly because that would draw attention to his illegal bugging of citizens. Hoover did intervene when Jack started an affair with a German-born twenty-seven-year-old named Ellen Rometsch. She met the president during one of his pool parties and they began an affair. Like a couple of other party girls Jack had been intimately involved with prior to his election, Ellen was a former member of the communist party. When the FBI became aware of their relationship, Hoover ordered an investigation, suspecting Rometsch was a spy. Kennedy quickly paid for Ellen to leave the country and return to Germany.

Hersh makes the subtle case that Kennedy's promiscuity may have indirectly contributed to his death. Two months before the assassination, Jack tore a groin muscle during a poolside sexual encounter. Afterward, he was forced to wear a stiff shoulder-to-groin brace that held his body in a rigid upright position in addition to his usual back brace. When Kennedy was shot in the neck by Oswald's first bullet, the new brace made it impossible for Jack to reflexively bend forward. Instead, he remained sitting straight up, allowing the second bullet to hit him directly in the head.

Private Lives Made Public

As much as Jackie enjoyed her solitude away from Washington, she was the consummate host at the White House. Just as they had been prior to his election, the Kennedys enjoyed socializing with colleagues and friends, some of whom regularly stayed over at the White House. Less welcome were relatives. Jackie's mother Janet was only invited on special occasions. Rose Kennedy was kept equally at bay, except when Jackie was out of town. Then Rose would act as a stand-in White House hostess. The only family members warmly welcomed were Jackie's sister Lee and her husband, Stas Radziwill.

Raising a Family in the White House

Jackie was particularly sensitive where Caroline and John were involved. She made a point of saying she did not want them to think they were official children. She fought to make their life in the White House as normal as possible under the circumstances. She requested that the doorman, for example, not rush over to open doors for them or treat them in any elevated manner. On the first day they arrived to move into the White House, Jackie had the groundskeepers build them a snowman to make the imposing mansion seem more friendly and homey.

Jackie and John F. Kennedy Jr.

Photo Credit: John F. Kennedy Presidential Library and Museum, Boston

As with every presidential family, there were reporters assigned to follow their every movement. The attention made it awkward and uncomfortable for Caroline to participate in her Georgetown playgroup. So Jackie brought the playgroup to the White House. She established a de facto nursery school. Jackie and the other mothers took turns either teaching or helping. The second year, licensed nursery and kindergarten teachers were hired to run what had become a classroom as well as playroom. Located in the solarium on the third floor of the White House, Jackie furnished the room with a sandbox, goldfish, guinea pigs, blackboards, paints, a homemade hatchery for chicks, and a teacher-approved library of books.

Jackie was equally solicitous of those who worked for her. When she learned that the Secret Service agents assigned to them had to work on Christmas, she insisted they bring their families along. She sent handwritten thank-you notes to the White House chef and his staff after every official or formal dinner. She tried hard to make the people who worked for the First Family feel appreciated. In return, she earned the respect and affection of nearly all who worked under her.

A Star Is Born

It didn't take the White House staff long to realize Jackie's popularity. Her social secretary, Letitia Baldrige, recalled that within the first month of the Kennedy administration, the White House was deluged with letters from women asking everything from what kind of shampoo did Jackie use to whether she wore curlers to bed. In one week alone more than 9,000 letters arrived.

Nancy Fleming, 1961's Miss America, said her wish was to be more like Jackie.

SHE SAID . . .

"I feel proud that my son has known the officers. It is my wish and my hope that some day he may be a man at least half as brave as the members of Brigade 2506."—English translation of Jackie Kennedy's remarks to the Cuban fighters

Composer Rudolph Friml wrote an operetta in homage to Jackie. An artist named Rene Cazussus carved a snow portrait of Jackie in a French mountainside. A quickie biography paperback about Jackie sold two million copies. A firm in Denmark manufactured Jackie mannequins. She was a pop culture phenomenon.

Jackie's Media Appeal

In the early 1960s, American women were starting to question traditional social norms. Many questioned why marriage and motherhood should prevent them from also establishing themselves outside the home. Women's magazines tapped into this disenchantment and increasingly featured articles about prominent women—and no one was more public than Jackie Kennedy, who became an icon to women who lived vicariously through her high-profile life.

Jackie Kennedy rides with her husband after arrival ceremonies for the president of Tunisia, 1961

Photo Credit: Abbie Rowe, National Park Service/John F. Kennedy Presidential Library and Museum, Boston

Although she was not classically beautiful, Jackie made the most of her looks by accentuating her best features, such as her smile and eyes. She was naturally photogenic, so magazine editors routinely wanted her to grace the covers of their magazines.

Unlike previous twentieth-century First Ladies, who were all older women—almost grandmotherly in demeanor—Jackie was a woman in her prime. She was also a celebrity, as popular as any Hollywood actress, so she was also regularly featured on movie and gossip magazines. She was in *Life* magazine so often the publication would later publish a book of the photos taken of her. Jackie appeared on the cover of *Life* magazine eleven times:

- **1953:** about her courtship with JFK
- **August 24, 1959:** dressed in a pink outfit and pearls
- **May 26, 1961:** wearing red and a pillbox hat
- **September 1961:** restoration work at the White House
- **December 6, 1963:** at JFK's funeral
- **April 26, 1963:** her childhood
- **November 17, 1967:** Jackie in Cambodia
- **November 1, 1968:** Jackie's marriage to Aristotle Onassis
- **March 31, 1972:** her troubles with photographer Ron Galella
- **July 1989:** a sixtieth birthday tribute
- **August 1999:** with Caroline

Jackie became the subject of countless media stories, some accurate, many not. A lot of the coverage centered on her wardrobe. Some of the more sensational publications went beyond reporting to speculation, rumor, and outright fabrication. One of the more persistent rumors was that Jackie bought Givenchy gowns but replaced the labels so it would appear that Oleg Cassini has designed them. Every new outfit was critiqued and offered as further evidence that Jackie was a shopaholic fixated on fashion. Frustrated, Jackie made it clear she personally found clothes a nuisance but felt obliged to be appropriately dressed.

In some ways the obsession over her wardrobe was Jackie's own doing. She was extremely reluctant to grant interviews and harbored a deep wariness of the media. By closing herself off, newspapers and magazines were left to fashion their own stories about her. So her wardrobe ended up getting more attention than it would have otherwise.

So did her children, which angered her. Protecting their privacy was a primary concern, and she frequently turned to White House press secretary Pierre Salinger to ensure that privacy. She was especially incensed after a magazine published unauthorized pictures of Caroline and John playing.

SHE SAID . . .

"I do not want to go down into coal mines or be the symbol of elegance. I will never be a committee woman or a club woman, because I'm not a joiner. I've always been the same person. I always felt I was myself. But with so many reporters watching, listening, how can anyone not seem like someone you're not?"

THEY SAID . . .

"Jackie referred to the women in the press corps as harpies. There was no question that she was brilliant and always ten jumps ahead of us. But Jackie was also very wary—in fact, I don't think she liked those of us in the press."

—White House reporter Helen Thomas

A Unique First Lady

While previous First Ladies confined themselves to overseeing the running of the White House household staff, Jack enlisted Jackie to share her opinion about political issues, although he never admitted this to the public out of fear it would generate controversy if it were widely known that a First Lady was involving herself in issues of national policy or security. Jackie regaled Jack with her usually astute opinion of political and military leaders, both domestic and foreign.

The Bay of Pigs

In 1961, a group of Cuban exiles, funded and trained by the United States, attempted to overthrow the government of Fidel Castro. The invasion, which took place at the Bay of Pigs, failed. More than 60 exiles were killed in the fighting, and 1,200 were captured and many were executed. Thousands of Cubans died. In December 1962, the surviving exiles were released in exchange for $53 million in medical necessities. They were greeted in Miami by the president and First Lady, and Jackie addressed them in perfect Spanish. "I feel proud that my son has known the officers. It is my wish and my hope that some day he may be a man at least half as brave as the members of Brigade 2506," she told them.

The President and First Lady greet members of the 2506 Cuban Invasion Brigade, 1962

Photo Credit: Cecil Stoughton, White House/John F. Kennedy Presidential Library and Museum, Boston

Charming Foreign Leaders

The charisma that made Jackie so photogenic also dazzled many of the dignitaries she met while accompanying the president on official business. On June 3, 1961, the Kennedys were at Schönbrunn Palace in Vienna for a dinner hosted by the Austrian president. Also in attendance was the Soviet premier, Nikita Khrushchev. Jackie was dressed in a shell-pink, silk-georgette chiffon evening dress embroidered with sequins. Photos from the evening show a dazzled Khrushchev. When photographers requested he pose with President Kennedy, the Soviet premier commented that he'd rather shake Jackie's hand first.

For his part, President Kennedy understood what a valuable asset his wife was, especially in international settings. While attending a dinner at the Palace of Versailles with French President Charles de Gaulle, Jackie wore a ravishing Givenchy silk gown and charmed de Gaulle with her flawless French. President Kennedy jokingly referred to himself as "the man who accompanied Jacqueline Kennedy to Paris."

Jack trusted his wife to be much more than just a goodwill ambassador, however. Unknown to the public, Jackie played an active role in administration diplomacy. Her interest in other cultures and her ability to speak several foreign languages made her the president's secret weapon. She acted as his translator at the Versailles dinner and gave speeches in Spanish promoting the Peace Corps during her visit to South America.

The First Lady addresses an audience at La Morita, Venezuela, 1961

Photo Credit: Cecil Stoughton, White House/John F. Kennedy Presidential Library and Museum, Boston

Jackie at the Taj Mahal in India, 1962

Photo Credit: Cecil Stoughton, White House/John F. Kennedy Presidential Library and Museum, Boston

In a highly unprecedented exhibition of First Lady diplomacy, Jackie wrote handwritten letters to leaders she met, including de Gaulle and India's prime minister, Jawaharlal Nehru. Her desire to protect what she felt was Kennedy's most important presidential accomplishment, the 1963 Nuclear Test Ban Treaty, led Jackie to write Soviet Premier Nikita Khrushchev just days after Kennedy's assassination. She asked him to remain committed to nuclear arms reduction and to encourage smaller nations to do likewise.

Like the president, Jackie used the power of television to promote his presidency. Prior to their trip to France, Jackie did an interview for French television that included a tour of the White House. Speaking in French, she pointed out the items and antiques in the White House that had been created by French artisans or been given as gifts by the French government.

QUESTION

What was the Nuclear Test Ban Treaty?

One of President Kennedy's primary goals was reaching an agreement with the Soviet Union regarding the nuclear arms race. In 1963, the two leaders signed the Limited Nuclear Test Ban Treaty, which prohibited nuclear tests in the atmosphere, in outer space, and underwater.

Patrick Bouvier Kennedy

In April 1963, the White House officially announced Jackie was pregnant. The baby would be the first child born to a sitting president in the twentieth century. After the announcement of her pregnancy, Jackie appeared in public just two times. That summer, Jack rented a secluded home on Squaw Island on Cape Cod. The president commuted between the cottage and Washington while Jackie rested and spent relaxed time with Caroline and John. Jack worried about her health and wanted her doctor on call at all times.

Although Jackie was not due until September, she went into labor on August 7. She was rushed to the hospital at Otis Air Force Base. Her obstetrician ordered an emergency casarean section. Although Jackie was in no danger, the baby was. Shortly before 1 P.M., Jackie gave birth to a four-pound, ten-ounce baby boy. He was named Patrick Bouvier Kennedy.

THEY SAID...

"My mother . . . knew she had been given the chance to play a part in history and worked hard to be worthy of the honor. When that period of her life came to an end she worked just as hard to ensure that the history of that time would be preserved and made available to future generations."

—Caroline Kennedy

The baby was having such a hard time breathing that the chaplain baptized him immediately. Despite his respiratory trouble, Patrick seemed in overall good health, and his prognosis was good. But not long after Jackie first held her son, his condition abruptly worsened. Patrick was transferred, first to Children's Hospital in Boston, then to Harvard's School of Public Health, where he was placed in a high-pressure oxygen chamber.

FACT

Patrick Bouvier Kennedy died from hyaline membrane disease (HMD), now called respiratory distress syndrome (RDS). It remains one of the most common afflictions in premature babies, whose undeveloped lungs are unable to function optimally. Typically the condition worsens over the first two to three days but usually improves with treatment.

Patrick died on August 9. Too weak to leave the hospital, Jackie did not attend his funeral, which was presided over by Kennedy family friend Cardinal Cushing. Although Jack and Jackie never spoke much about Patrick's death, it was clear to those around the couple that his death brought them closer together. Unlike the death of Arabella, which had driven a wedge between the two of them because Jack had not been there for Jackie, this death was a shared loss. When Jackie was released from the hospital on August 14, the normally reserved Kennedys walked out hand in hand. Jackie convalesced at Squaw Island, so Jack commuted to Cape Cod several times a week to be with her.

The Kennedy family with their dogs on Squaw Island, 1963

Cecil Stoughton, White House/John F. Kennedy Presidential Library and Museum, Boston

Lee Radziwill had been sailing as a guest on Aristotle Onassis's yacht when she heard about Patrick. She rushed to her sister and spent a week with her at Squaw Island. Lee suggested to Onassis that it might be good for Jackie to join them on the cruise, and Jackie accepted the subsequent invitation.

In mid-November, Jackie made her first public appearance since Patrick's death. It was time to look forward. The 1964 election year was quickly approaching, and soon it would be time to go back on the campaign trail. With that in mind, Jackie agreed to accompany her husband on a political trip to Texas, where he hoped to gain support for a second term.

Chapter 12

A NATION MOURNS

John F. Kennedy was the fourth American president to be assassinated but the first to be killed in the age of modern technology. News of the tragedy was broadcast around the world within minutes of the shooting. In the aftermath, people all over the country sat riveted in front of their televisions as a young widow with two small children buried her husband. The images of Jackie from those days left an indelible mark on the minds and hearts of Americans for decades to come.

Fateful Trip to Dallas

A couple of months after Patrick Kennedy's death, the president began finalizing plans for a trip to Texas to drum up support for his civil rights initiatives. With the 1964 presidential election just a year away, the swing through Texas gave Kennedy an opportunity to do some early campaigning. Believing Jackie was recovered enough to return to the public spotlight—and realizing how much of an asset she was—Jack asked her to accompany him. Whether out of duty or guilt over his displeasure at her socializing with Onassis, Jackie accepted. Although she did not like going on political trips, she promised to be wherever he wanted her to be.

Traveling with the President

Franklin Delano Roosevelt was the first commander in chief to fly in office. Former military man Dwight Eisenhower made flying a regular aspect of his administration. He primarily used propeller planes but toward the end of his second term became the first president to fly in a jet, the Boeing 707. But the presidency came fully into the jet age with Kennedy, who began flying a specially modified 707 in October 1962.

> **FACT**
> The aircraft used by the president is supplied and maintained by the U.S. Air Force. Although a plane is officially only designated *Air Force One* when the president is on board, the term is commonly used to designate the actual planes reserved for his use. The vice president's designation is *Air Force Two*.

Initially, the Air Force had painted Kennedy's presidential plane in red and metallic gold, with the United States of America printed in block letters. Kennedy thought the design and colors were too regal in appearance. So at Jackie's suggestion, his administration contacted French-born designer Raymond Loewy, who used the Declaration of Independence as his inspiration. He recreated the way the country's name was printed on the document: all upper-case in a typeface called Caslon. He then suggested painting the plane slate blue, a color associated with early America, and the more modern cyan blue to represent the present and future of the country. He left the bottom of the plane's fuselage silver and added the presidential seal to both sides of the plane near its nose. The last flourish was the American flag painted on the tail. Loewy's design was a public and critical success and helped *Air Force One* become an icon recognized the world over.

Warm Welcome

On November 21, 1963, the president and First Lady left Andrews Air Force Base and made a brief stop in San Antonio. From there, they flew to Houston, where they toured the NASA facility, which was already deeply involved with the race to send a man to the moon. They checked into the Rice Hotel, where they were scheduled to make an appearance at a meeting of the League of United Latin-American Citizens. After Kennedy gave his speech, Jackie took to the stage and briefly addressed the crowd in Spanish. Despite her nervousness, she earned cheers from the crowd. From there they went to a dinner honoring Congressman Albert Thomas before returning to *Air Force One*. They touched down in Fort Worth a little after 11:00 P.M. That evening, Jack told Jackie and several advisors that Dallas was nut country, and he alluded to the possibility of someone trying to shoot him. Whether it was an actual premonition or just a bad joke, it was a comment nobody would ever forget.

It was drizzling in Fort Worth the morning of November 22. But a crowd of supporters and curiosity seekers had started gathering outside the president's hotel before dawn. When Kennedy exited to speak to the crowd, several people shouted out wondering where Jackie was. He joked that she was still getting ready, adding that it was worth it because she always looked better than anyone else when she finally arrived.

When Jackie entered the ballroom for a breakfast with the Fort Worth Chamber of Commerce, she received a standing ovation. No doubt understanding that she acted as a buffer against the political tensions her husband had to deal with, she later promised Jack that she would accompany him on whatever trips he wanted her to. They made plans to fly to California together two weeks later.

Indelible Images

It was sunny in Dallas when *Air Force One* touched down at Love Field shortly before noon. Originally, the forecast had been for cool weather, so Jackie was dressed in a pink wool suit and a matching pillbox hat. When he heard the weather was supposed to be sunny and warm, the president requested that the top be removed from his motorcade car, claiming he wanted to show Jackie off to all the Texans.

The presidential motorcade left Love Field and headed toward the Trade Mart where Kennedy was scheduled to speak. One of Kennedy's aides, Dave Powers, instructed Jackie to wave and make eye contact with spectators on her side of the car—if she and the president both looked in the same direction, it would be a wasted opportunity. They drove through the streets of Dallas in the back of the open car, with Texas Governor John Connally and his wife in the front. It was so bright that Jackie put on her sunglasses, but Jack told her to take them off. Those were the last words he would ever say to her.

As the motorcade proceeded through Dealey Plaza, Jackie heard a terrible noise and initially assumed it was a motorcycle backfiring.

SHE SAID . . .

"Every time we got off the plane that day, three times they gave me the yellow roses of Texas. But in Dallas they gave me red roses. I thought how funny, red roses—so all the seat was full of blood and red roses."

She heard Governor Connally cry out, and then she saw Jack turn toward her, his hand to his throat. She later recalled he looked puzzled and then slumped forward. According to the official record, the first bullet entered the back of Kennedy's neck, exited through his throat and struck Connally, who was sitting in the front seat. The second bullet took off a large portion of the president's head. Videos and photographs show Jackie climbing out onto the trunk of the car. Later, she claimed to have no recollection of it. The motorcade sped to the Parkland Hospital with Jackie cradling her husband's head in her lap the entire way. She recalled attempting to hold the top of his head down to stop the bleeding and prevent the brain from leaking out. She knew, though, it was a futile gesture. John Fitzgerald Kennedy was dead.

After doctors officially pronounced the president dead, Jackie spent time with his body and put her wedding ring in Jack's casket. Heading back to *Air Force One* to accompany the body back to Washington, she refused to change out of her bloodied clothes, insisting the nation see exactly what had been done to her husband. The photograph of her standing next to Lyndon Johnson as he is sworn in as president on *Air Force One* was nothing short of shattering.

Jacqueline Kennedy stands by Lyndon Johnson as Judge Sarah T. Hughes administers the presidential oath of office aboard *Air Force One* at Love Field in Dallas, Texas, 1963

Photo Credit: Cecil Stoughton, White House/John F. Kennedy Presidential Library and Museum, Boston

Accused Assassin

Minutes after the shooting, Dallas police zeroed in on the Texas School Book Depository as a place where a sniper could have fired on the motorcade. A short time later, police received a call that Officer J. D. Tippett had been shot and killed. Later that afternoon, police swarmed into a movie theater and arrested Lee Harvey Oswald for Tippett's murder. He quickly became a suspect in the president's death after investigators discovered he was the only employee who had left the Texas School Book Depository after the assassination.

Early Life

Lee Harvey Oswald was born in New Orleans October 18, 1939, two months after his father Robert suffered a fatal heart attack. When he was three, his mother Marguerite placed Lee and his brothers in a Lutheran orphanage. He stayed there for nearly two years until Marguerite took him with her to Dallas, where she married her third husband, Edwin Ekdahl, in 1944. His brothers stayed in military school. The couple divorced in 1948, and Lee moved with his mother to New York City when he was twelve years old. They rented a small apartment in the Bronx and Marguerite found work in a dress shop. She worked a twelve-hour day, leaving Lee to make his own meals and fend for himself. A small, almost scrawny youth, Lee lived a solitary existence, killing time at the library or local museums. But mostly he rode the subway aimlessly for hours on end.

Although he was enrolled in the eighth grade, Lee was chronically truant and at one point stayed away from school for two months. Eventually, he was caught by a truant officer and taken to juvenile court. He was sentenced to a detention center for a three-week psychiatric evaluation. His social worker, Evelyn Siegel, determined he was not mentally disturbed; just an emotionally distant boy who was distrustful of others. That said, she also labeled him as possessing a "personality pattern disturbance with schizoid features and passive-aggressive tendencies." But the determination wasn't enough to keep him incarcerated or hospitalized.

A Communist Sympathizer

According to diary entries, Oswald's political awakening occurred when he read a leaflet protesting the pending executions of Julius and Ethel Rosenberg, who had been convicted of being Soviet spies. He found a sense of purpose in opposing the status quo—a system that had largely ignored and abandoned him. He began reading every book he could find on socialism he could find in the local libraries.

After Oswald was apprehended a second time for truancy, breaking terms of his earlier probation, Marguerite and Lee left New York for New Orleans and settled in a seedy neighborhood adjacent to the French Quarter. His nomadic life had left him rootless and volatile—Lee was known to hit his mother and had threatened some members of his family with a knife. Searching for a sense of belonging, he enlisted in the marines at age seventeen. But all he found was more estrangement.

While in the service, Oswald earned a sharpshooting rating but he quickly ran afoul of regulations. A year after enlisting, he accidentally shot himself with an unauthorized pistol and was court-martialed. He then was court-martialed and jailed after attacking an officer. He left the marines, saying his mother was in poor health and needed him to look after her.

Defection to the Soviet Union

When he was nineteen, Oswald emigrated to the Soviet Union. While proclaiming himself to be a dedicated Marxist, acquaintances of his in Russia claim he showed no interest in communism. He seemed to arouse suspicion among both Soviet and American intelligence officials with whom he had contact.

In the Soviet Union, he met a woman named Marina Prusakova. The two married, had a daughter, and returned to the United States in 1962. Oswald went through a series of jobs before finding employment at the Texas School Book Depository in October 1963.

November 1963

Police questioned Oswald for two days after Kennedy's assassination, but Oswald never confessed to anything. On November 24, Oswald was fatally shot by nightclub owner Jack Ruby as he was being transferred to the Dallas County Jail.

Was Oswald a Russian spy, a double agent, an angry outcast looking to make a statement or name for himself? Nobody knows for absolute sure. Was he a lone gunman acting on his own or part of a conspiracy? Nobody knows that for sure, either. The suspicious circumstances surrounding Oswald's life and the unanswered questions about the president's death, made Jackie's tragedy that much more profound in the eyes of the public.

The Funeral

While on *Air Force One* en route from Dallas to Washington, Jackie placed a phone call to senior members of the White House staff to discuss funeral arrangements and accompanying ceremonies. Jackie was inspired by the way the East Room of the White House had been decorated during Lincoln's funeral and had the aides contact an upholsterer to have the windows and chandelier in the East Room draped with the black fabric. She also wanted the ceremony to be simple, like Lincoln's. Having the funeral to focus on was a way for Jackie to deal with the initial shock and grief of the assassination. Bobby Kennedy met Jackie when *Air Force One* landed in Washington, D.C. She stayed in her bloodied pink suit until dawn the next morning.

THEY SAID...

"She was absolutely stoic during the entire time. Most of us journalists felt that she knew about Jack's philandering, and the consensus was that there had been huge fights between them. But Jackie was crazy about him and his death very nearly destroyed her."

—Muriel Dobbin

Jackie and Bobby planned Jack's funeral together, although it was clearly Jackie who took the lead, supervising every aspect of Jack's burial. She directed the florist to pick flowers from the magnolia tree in the South Lawn. Andrew Johnson had planted it in memory of Abraham Lincoln. Jackie wanted Jack's funeral to echo Lincoln's not just because both men had been assassinated but because she believed Jack had been as much of a visionary as Lincoln had been, and that vision had played a part in his death.

QUESTION
Where did the tradition of the riderless horse come from?
The tradition of a riderless horse dates back to fourteenth century Mongolia, when a horse was sacrificed to accompany a fallen warrior to the next life. In modern times, a riderless horse is used in army and marine funerals. Abraham Lincoln was the first U.S. president to be honored with a riderless horse at his funeral in 1865. Ironically, the riderless horse at Kennedy's funeral was named Black Jack.

On Saturday, November 23, the president's body lay in state at the White House; on Sunday, in the Capitol Rotunda. His closed coffin was draped with an American flag. President Johnson placed a wreath by the casket and dignitaries gave eulogies. Jackie brought Caroline and together they knelt to pray, Caroline reaching under the flag to touch her father's coffin. That same day, millions of Americans watched in shock as Lee Harvey Oswald was murdered on live TV by a Dallas nightclub owner, Jack Ruby.

John F. Kennedy was buried on Monday, November 25, 1963. Jackie and her two children were accompanied by Bobby and Ted Kennedy as they walked behind the horse-drawn caisson that carried Jack's coffin and the riderless horse with empty boots reversed in hanging stirrups.

The funeral service was held at St. Matthew's Cathedral. Instead of burying Jack in Boston, Jackie chose to have him interred at

SHE SAID . . .

"I have nothing else to do in life now except to raise my children well, to help them move forward through this terrible thing—otherwise they will be tied forever to their father's death. I have to make sure they survive."

Arlington National Cemetery, explaining, "He belongs to the people." As the coffin passed by, Jackie leaned over and whispered to her son, who raised his hand in a salute to his father. Jackie kept her composure through the burial. While a formation of fifty fighter jets flew overhead, she lit the eternal flame beside Jack's grave. A twenty-one gun salute was followed by a lone bugler playing the mournful notes of "Taps." After the flag on the coffin was folded and handed to Jackie, the coffin was lowered into the ground.

Jackie, Caroline, and John Jr. depart the Capitol building

Photo Credit: Abbie Rowe, National Park Service/John F. Kennedy Presidential Library and Museum, Boston

Jackie leaves the burial site at Arlington National Cemetery

Photo Credit: John F. Kennedy Presidential Library and Museum, Boston

Putting National Interests First

Jackie understood that her husband's assassination was more than just a personal tragedy; it was a national trauma. It was also history. Jackie seemed determined to give her husband's senseless death meaning and to maintain dignity at all costs.

Jackie personally greeted every dignitary who came to pay respects. She wrote personal notes to each of the 114 staff members. She appeared on television to thank the hundreds of thousands of people who had sent their condolences. Less than a week after Jack's funeral, Jackie went through his belongings and personal effects. She selected various items to give as gifts to each member of his cabinet as a memento of their service with the president.

Some people raised a curious eyebrow when Jackie celebrated John Jr.'s birthday the night of his father's funeral and Caroline's a couple of days later. But it wasn't denial or the manic actions of a woman on the edge of an emotional breakdown. Instead, it was a clear-eyed choice intended to honor and celebrate Jack's memory as a loving father. His children were his ultimate legacy, and Jackie wanted them—and the world—to remember that. More important, Jackie did not want her children's lives forever informed or shaped by their father's death. Life needed to go on.

THEY SAID...

"Truly noble women and men have somehow learned how to speak and act in ways that are appropriate at the moment, no matter what their personal feelings or needs. . . . The country needed her to hold all people together . . . she let no one down. Her sense of history, her dignity and her refusal to think only of herself . . . brought order to the chaos."

—Donald Spoto, *Jacqueline Bouvier Kennedy Onassis*

Government mandate requires that an outgoing president must vacate the White House so that the incoming president can immediately move in. However, because Jackie needed to arrange a place to live, she lived in the White House for two weeks. She and the children finally moved out on December 6 and into a home in Georgetown. Before leaving, she placed an inscription on the mantel in the Lincoln bedroom she had shared with Jack that read, "In this room lived John Fitzgerald Kennedy with his wife Jacqueline during the two years, ten months, and two days he was President of the United States." Pat Nixon removed the plaque when she and Richard Nixon moved into the White House after his 1968 victory.

The Birth of Camelot

A week after Jack's murder, on November 29, Jackie called journalist Theodore White and requested he come meet her at Hyannis Port where she had spent a somber Thanksgiving with the Kennedy clan. White had published *The Making of the President*, a Pulitzer Prize–winning book about the 1960 presidential campaign, and Jackie apparently trusted him. She wanted to speak to the American public, she wanted to do so in the pages of *Life* magazine, and she wanted White to write the article.

SHE SAID . . .

"At night before we'd go to sleep . . . Jack liked to play some records. And the song he loved most came at the very end of this record, the last side of *Camelot* . . . 'Don't let it be forgot, that once there was a spot, for one brief shining moment that was known as Camelot.' There'll never be another Camelot again."

White arrived later that evening and they spoke alone for several hours. White later said that Jackie didn't want to leave her husband's legacy in the hands of historians or journalists. Although it was never spoken of directly, Jackie knew of her husband's womanizing and philandering and that was not what she wanted him remembered for. She wanted his legacy to be about the hope and charisma he brought to the presidency.

Jackie told White that when Jack was a young boy he fantasized about being a great Knight, like those of King Arthur's Round Table, and performing great deeds. That's why one of his favorite musicals was Lerner and Loewe's *Camelot*. In the same way that Jack used the media to promote himself and win over voters in the 1960 presidential race, Jackie used the press to help spin the mythology she thought fitting for her husband's life of public service.

Her efforts were calculated and specific. She was able to persuade President Johnson to change the name of Cape Canaveral in Florida to Cape Kennedy, in honor of Jack's unrelenting support of the space program and his challenge to the nation to land a man on the moon. Through her efforts and lobbying there was a special tribute to Kennedy at the 1964 Democratic Convention. Jackie also began work on planning a John F. Kennedy Memorial Library in Boston, Massachusetts. Her husband's legacy, and her children, became her purpose.

In 1965, author William Manchester approached Jackie about writing a book on the assassination. She approved and granted Manchester more than five hours of interviews. But when the publisher sold the serialization rights of *The Death of a President* to *Look* magazine in 1966, Jackie accused Manchester of commercializing the assassination. Perhaps more to the point, she was upset with some of the anecdotes Manchester included in the book, such as a passage that mentioned the way Jackie allegedly checked the mirror to see if she had wrinkles. She was upset enough to go to court and seek an injunction to stop the book from being published. Manchester ultimately agreed to make some minor changes in the manuscript and donated a larger percentage of the book's earnings to the Kennedy Library. The suit was dropped, and the image of Camelot was perpetuated.

The Strange Bouvier Connection to Oswald

It was pure coincidence that an acquaintance of Jackie's mother had befriended Lee Harvey Oswald in the years just prior to the assassination. George de Mohrenschildt was a Russian-born society figure and petroleum geologist. After the Bolsheviks seized power, George's family fled to Poland, where he grew up. He earned a degree in international commerce at the University of Liége and immigrated to America in May 1938. George spent that summer with his older brother Dimitri on Long Island, where he got a job selling perfume. It was during that time that he befriended Janet Bouvier. He also became close friends with Black Jack's sister Edith. When he first met Jackie, she was just turning nine years old.

From 1939 to 1941, George worked in the insurance industry. De Mohrenschildt later claimed he also gathered information on pro-German people and companies operating in the United States on behalf of French intelligence prior to World War II. After failing to pass his broker's test, George made a documentary film about Polish resistance fighters. He applied to the OSS after Pearl Harbor but was rejected. His brother, Dimitri, however, was accepted and helped establish Radio Free Europe.

After the war ended, de Mohrenschildt settled in Dallas, Texas. He received a master's degree in petroleum geology from the University of Texas and became a U.S. citizen in 1949. A well-known member of Dallas's expatriate Russian community, George worked for a number of oil companies and taught at a local college. In June 1959 he married a former dancer named Jeanne Fomenko, who had also been born in Russia but was then a naturalized U.S. citizen.

THEY SAID...

"Mrs. Bouvier . . . was in the process of getting a divorce from her husband. I met him also. We were very close friends. We saw each other every day. I met Jackie then, when she was a little girl; she was a very strong-willed child, very intelligent and very attractive child."

—George de Mohrenschildt

The Oswalds

In 1962, Jackie agreed to become the honorary chairwoman of a cystic fibrosis foundation founded by de Mohrenschildt in memory of his late son Sergei, who had died of the disease. In the summer of that same year, George met Lee Harvey Oswald and his wife Marina, who spoke very limited English. George and Jeanne introduced them to other members of the area's Russian community and tried to help Lee find a job. They also took Marina under their wing because Oswald routinely beat her. For a brief while, Marina moved in with George's daughter but ultimately went back to her husband.

In June 1963, de Mohrenschildt moved to Haiti to work on some oil projects. After Kennedy was assassinated, he testified before the Warren Commission in 1964 about his relationship with Oswald. In subsequent years, George would accuse the CIA of harassing and watching him because of his association with Oswald.

FACT

The President's Commission on the Assassination of President Kennedy was established to investigate John F. Kennedy's death. Known unofficially as the Warren Commission after its chairman, Chief Justice Earl Warren, the commission published its 888-page report in 1964. Based on testimony and depositions from 553 witnesses and more than 3,000 exhibits, the Commission voted four to three that Oswald acted alone.

On November 9, 1976, Jeanne had de Mohrenschildt committed to a mental institution in Texas for three months. She told doctors her husband suffered from depression, heard voices, and saw visions. She also claimed George had tried suicide on four different occasions. A month after his release from the hospital, George went back to work. He returned from a business trip to Belgium on March 16, 1977, deeply depressed. He contacted journalist Edward Jay Epstein, who had written articles critical of the Warren Commission's findings. De Mohrenschildt agreed to give Epstein an interview for $4,000, intended for publication in *Reader's Digest*. During a break in the interview, George received a communication from an investigator who worked for the House Select Committee on Assassinations, which had been convened to investigate the killings of John F. Kennedy and Dr. Martin Luther King. That same afternoon, de Mohrenschildt committed suicide with a shotgun.

Chapter 13

STARTING OVER

As First Lady, Jackie exuded confidence and composure. She was a woman comfortable in her skin who knew where her life was going and what was expected of her. Then that future was ripped out from under her, leaving her uncertain, vulnerable, and emotionally adrift.

Seclusion

As traumatized as the nation was in the wake of the president's assassination, the shock and horror eventually faded from the public's psyche. Despite the lingering sense that the president's murder presaged a wind of change, life went on. But for Jackie, the loss only grew as the daily reality of her husband's absence deepened. The Camelot myth she went to such pains to promote was a kind of wish fulfillment—the longed-for life and legacy she had imagined she and Jack would have left if they had been given the time. Plus, it was important to Jackie that her children grow up believing the best about their father.

Privacy

But the composed, brave image she had projected in the immediate aftermath of the assassination crumbled behind closed doors. Jackie expressed her sense of helplessness and futility to friends. She suffered grievous bouts of weeping and compulsively bit her nails. Family members and others lent as much support as she would allow. Bobby Kennedy became a surrogate father to Caroline and John Jr. Jackie's mother and sister visited her almost daily and kept her company in the evenings. The Johnsons invited her to dinner, but the thought of going back to the White House was too painful for Jackie, so she declined. After her appearance on national television to thank the public for their cards, letters, and general outpouring of support, Jackie would rarely ever speak publicly about herself.

Partly out of compassion and partly self-serving, Jackie had her choice of professional opportunities. President Johnson offered her the position of Ambassador to France. Some Democrats

SHE SAID . . .

"Sometimes I wake in the morning, eager to tell him something, and he's not there. Nearly every religion teaches there's an afterlife, and I cling to that hope. Those three years in the White House were really the happiest time for us, the closest, and now it's all gone. Now there is nothing."

floated the idea of her running for political office. Had she wanted it, a newspaper column or television show was hers for the taking. Jackie rejected every suggestion and offer. She was too emotionally distracted to focus on anything but raising her children and protecting her husband's image.

Financial Matters

Jack's will stipulated that his estate be divided into two trusts, one to be shared by his children, the other to go to Jackie. Her annual income from the trust was $200,000—or the equivalent of $1.29 million today. Jackie should have been able to live very comfortably and not worry about money for the rest of her life. But her restlessness in the months and years following Jack's death often found release in the form of shopping. While she spent lavishly on herself, she also became frugal with her employees. She reportedly refused to pay overtime to her personal attendant, and she declined to give her secretary, Mary Gallagher, a raise, even though her $12,000 salary came out of the $50,000 given by the government. Jackie also dismissed Jack's longtime personal secretary, Evelyn Lincoln, who had worked for Kennedy since 1953 and was helping gather and organize material for the Kennedy library.

FACT
After the assassination, Congress voted to pay for all funeral expenses and allotted Jackie a $50,000 budget for staff and office expenses for the next two years. She was also granted free postage privileges and a year of Secret Service protection. She was also entitled to a $10,000 annual widow's pension for life or until she remarried.

Seemingly unable to settle herself, Jackie was constantly on the move, traveling to Europe on ski trips or cruises in the Mediterranean. Back home, she fluttered back and forth between Georgetown and Hyannis Port. Through it all the media—and the public—followed her every action.

Move to New York

After leaving the White House Jackie decided to stay in the Washington, D.C., area and bought a large Colonial-style house for $175,000. The grace under pressure Jackie exhibited in the aftermath of the assassination solidified her popularity and made her an international icon. According to polls taken at the time, Jacqueline Kennedy was the most admired person in the world. But with the admiration came notoriety—and a loss of privacy. Tour buses made regular stops at the house so their passengers could take photos, hoping for a glimpse of Jackie or her children. Some were bold enough to ring the doorbell. Others set up picnic tables across the street and peered through binoculars. The relentless attention finally became too much to bear. In July 1964, just four months after moving in, it was announced that Jackie was selling the Georgetown house as well as the Wexford estate and moving to New York City.

A New Residence

Jackie let go of both Mary Gallagher and Providencia Paredes, who went to work for Bobby Kennedy. She hired longtime friend Nancy Tuckerman and press secretary Pam Turnure to staff the New York office. After the announcement, Jackie returned to the Washington house just two more times. Her life in the nation's capital was over.

> ## THEY SAID...
> "Going back to our childhood days, she always loved New York and everything about it—the museums, the park, the people. She was always drawn back to New York. She chose to bring her children up in the city."
>
> —Nancy Tuckerman

Jackie bought a fifteen-room apartment at 1040 Fifth Avenue for $250,000. She had a spectacular view of the Metropolitan Museum of Art and Central Park. Her sister lived nearby, but most important for Jackie was that living in a wealthy area inhabited by the social elite meant she wouldn't be gawked at. She intended to blend into her well-heeled surroundings and find a measure of privacy. Bobby Kennedy, who had become her closest companion, bought an apartment at United Nations Plaza. While many assumed it was to be close to Jackie and the children, it was primarily because Bobby was planning a run for the Senate and needed to establish New York residency.

SHE SAID . . .

"It is nearly a year since he has been gone. He was so full of love and life. . . . 'Now I think I should have known he was magic all along. I did know it—but I should have guessed it could not last. So now he is a legend when he would have preferred to be a man.'"—Jacqueline Kennedy, quoting Guinevere from *Camelot*

1964

While the increased anonymity of Manhattan comforted Jackie, she still struggled with the loss of her husband. She spent 1964 in mourning. Caroline once mentioned to her schoolteacher that her mother cried a lot of the time. It was impossible for Jackie to get away from the assassination, and that was particularly difficult for her. In March she testified before the Warren Commission, and throughout the year magazines and newspapers ran countless articles about it. As November approached Jackie canceled her newspapers.

To mark the anniversary of his death, Jackie agreed to cooperate with *Look* magazine on a memorial issue. She posed for pictures with her children and wrote a tribute to her late husband for the issue. She worked with the editors on layout and helped select photos of Jack to accompany quotations she had picked out. But as the end of 1964 neared, it appeared Jackie was as emotionally raw as she had been in the days following Jack's death. She wondered how she would ever be normal again.

The Warhol Portraits

Jackie's grief inspired compassion, pity, admiration—and art. Andy Warhol, a successful commercial illustrator, became one of the most influential artists of the twentieth century by using popular culture as his canvas. In the early 1960s, Warhol began producing paintings featuring famous and iconographic American products, such as Campbell's Soup cans, and celebrities, including Marilyn Monroe and Elizabeth Taylor. He also used newspaper photographs of current events. During the summer of 1962, he created *129 Die in Jet*, based on a photograph run by the *New York Mirror* that showed the wreckage of a fatal plane crash. From that point on, he frequently used death as an underlying theme in his work.

The Monroe Portraits

After Marilyn Monroe's death on August 5, 1962, Warhol used a publicity photo Gene Korman had taken of Monroe on the set of the film *Niagara* in 1953, cropped it to fit the canvas he was working on, and silkscreened it. It would become his signature style.

QUESTION
What is silkscreening?
To silkscreen an image, Warhol enlarged a photograph and transferred it in glue onto silk fabric. He then rolled ink across it so that the ink went through the silk but not the glue. That resulted in images that were essentially the same but still unique because each was slightly different due to the inking process.

He followed the Marilyn portraits with a series of suicide paintings. He scoured old newspaper clippings, magazines, and photograph collections for images of suicide. By November 1963, Warhol was working on a new series called *Death and Disaster*. The Kennedy assassination reaffirmed Warhol's view that the news media was morbidly fascinated with death and equally obsessed with celebrity. After the assassination turned Jackie into a symbol of national grief, it was inevitable that Warhol would find Jackie an irresistible subject. He was especially intrigued by her ability to spin the media in creating the Camelot mythology.

Flash—November 22, 1963

In late 1963, Warhol began painting a series of small portraits depicting Jackie as the grieving widow. He produced hundreds of paintings that illustrated how Jackie had become an icon through the tragedy. He also produced a series of eleven screen prints, complete with text, titled *Flash—November 22, 1963*, that recreated news wire copy. The *Flash* series examines the media coverage of the assassination and its aftermath, which Warhol construed as a barrage on the senses.

Although Warhol was considered a provocateur, challenging and expanding the notion of what exactly art is, he was also an astute observer and his canvases now reflect the changing social climate and mores of the country. One of his more powerful series was based on photographs of police dogs attacking civil rights demonstrators in Birmingham, Alabama. The two series featuring Jackie were equally perceptive in that he used her as the symbol of an event that would forever change America.

THEY SAID...

"What's great about this country is that America started the tradition where the richest consumers buy essentially the same things as the poorest. You can be watching TV and see Coca Cola, and you know that the President drinks Coca Cola, Liz Taylor drinks Coca Cola, and just think, you can drink Coca Cola, too. . . . All the Cokes are the same, and all the Cokes are good."

—Andy Warhol, *The Philosophy of Andy Warhol:*
(From A to B and Back Again)

Life after JFK

Although Jackie loved New York, she was accustomed to spending the summer months away from the city. But instead of heading back to Newport, East Hampton, or Hyannis Port, Jackie chose a ten-room home in rural, woodsy Bernardsville, New Jersey. She liked the area because she could enjoy the outdoors with her children and there were plenty of riding paths.

Although the New York apartment was tastefully done, her primary objective was to make a permanent home for herself and her children. Without Jack there to act as a buffer, Jackie felt like an outsider among the Kennedy clan, except for Bobby. Her brother-in-law became her confidant. At one point, Jackie actually considered sending her children to stay with Bobby, concerned her unrelenting grief was adversely affecting them. Being older, Caroline suffered the loss of her father more than John Jr. did, and she was frequently withdrawn. But around Bobby she would open up, and she enjoyed a warm relationship with him.

SHE SAID . . .

"Because John Kennedy was so involved in life, his library will be not just a repository of papers and relics of the past. It will also be a vital center of education and exchange and thought, which will grow and change with the times. . . . It will be, we hope, not only a memorial to President Kennedy but a living center of study of the times in which he lived, which will inspire the ideals of democracy and freedom in young people all over the world."

New Romance

Once she was settled with her family in her New York apartment, Jackie finally began to finally emerge from her crippling grief. She threw small, intimate dinner parties for a select group of friends. Eventually, she discreetly sought out romance. One of her first relationships as a widow was with architect Jack Warnecke, whom she worked with to design Jack's grave at Arlington. Although their affair lasted eighteen months, she and Warnecke never appeared in public as a couple. Part of the reason was Jackie's obsession with privacy; another part was concern over the potential public reaction to her relationship with another man less than a year after her husband's death.

> **FACT**
> Located in Virginia, Arlington National Cemetery honors Armed Forces veterans and selected prominent civilians. More than 300,000 people are buried there, and 5,000 people are laid to rest there each year. John F. Kennedy is one of only two presidents to be interred at Arlington National Cemetery. The other is William Howard Taft.

John F. Kennedy Presidential Library and Museum

Jackie was the driving force behind the John F. Kennedy Presidential Library and Museum. She was extremely hands-on and oversaw everything from the organization of the exhibits to the location and design of the building. One of Jackie's most important relationships in the years after Jack's death was with architect I. M. Pei. It was deeply personal and purely platonic. Pei was the man to whom she entrusted the design of the building. Jackie chose Pei over other better-known architects because he impressed her with his individualistic style. She also felt he had the right temperament and emotional connection to the project, so his relative inexperience did not concern her. Perhaps most telling is that she once commented that she saw in Pei great untapped potential, which reminded her of the young Jack.

Jackie wanted a venue that would not only honor Jack's legacy of public service but also foster the passion behind public service. She wanted a forum where ideas were exchanged and intellectual conversations stimulated. In other words, she wanted the kind of place in which her French heroine, Juliette de Récamier, would have felt at home. Through those efforts, the Institute of Politics, later known as the Kennedy School of Government at Harvard, was established.

Campaigning for Bobby

After Jack's death, Bobby Kennedy seriously considered dropping out of politics, but Jackie urged him not to. Convinced he owed it to himself and his brother's memory to go on, Bobby laid out his political goals. When Jack was alive, they had already discussed plans for Bobby to run for the Democratic presidential nomination in 1968. Now that Jack was gone, Bobby decided to resign his position as attorney general and confided to Jackie that he wanted to run for the U.S. Senate in New York. Jackie supported Bobby's aspiration unconditionally and was willing to help him any way she could. Just as she had done with Jack, she gave Bobby books to read she thought would inspire him and offered him literary allusions for his speeches. During the 1964 Democratic Convention, Jackie appeared on his behalf at a reception. She introduced him to influential people she knew through her family contacts. That November, Bobby won the Senate election by a wide margin.

In turn, Bobby made Jackie more politically conscious, particularly about the war in Vietnam, which he strongly opposed. As Bobby became more vocally critical of Lyndon Johnson and the war, Jackie developed her own negative opinion of the war, primarily based on the suffering war caused to the Vietnamese people and the soldiers fighting there. One day her friend Kitty Carlisle Hart, who was on the board of the Red Cross, asked Jackie if she wanted to help with wounded soldiers who had been flown directly from the battlefield to a veterans' hospital in Queens. Jackie went and spent the day talking to the wounded and dying. Afterward, her depression and despair had noticeably lifted. She told a friend that getting back out in the world reminded her that there are other people who had been through much worse than she had endured.

Rumors

There is no definitive evidence that Jackie and Bobby were anything more than close friends, but there were inevitable rumors that they were lovers. Some Kennedy biographers and personal friends insist they became intimately involved after the assassination; or, more precisely, that they shared a sexually intimate friendship as well as a deep emotional attachment. Others believe they were simply bonded by the death of a loved one. Whatever the case, there's no denying they spent considerable time together and shared a profound affection for one another. It was Bobby who urged Jackie to throw dinner parties when all she wanted to do was lock herself away and give in to her depression. He organized a surprise party for her thirty-fifth birthday in July 1964. He made time to spend with her when he was in Manhattan, and Jackie came to rely and depend on Bobby both practically and emotionally.

Robert Kennedy's Assassination

Bobby entered the primary race late. At the beginning of the primaries, Senator Eugene McCarthy was the only Democrat to challenge the sitting president for the Democratic nomination, and he ran on an antiwar platform. The New Hampshire primary went well for McCarthy, who pulled in 42 percent of the vote and came in a close second to Johnson's 49 percent. Four days later, Bobby announced his candidacy. McCarthy supporters felt betrayed by Kennedy, and the two candidates became bitter rivals.

FACT

Martin Luther King was standing on the balcony of the Lorraine Motel in Memphis when he was shot at 6:01 P.M. on April 4, 1968. His assassination sparked riots in more than 100 American cities. Thirty-nine people died during the riots, and more than 2,500 others were injured. More than 300,000 mourners attended his funeral.

When Bobby officially announced he was running for the presidency, Jackie came out publicly in support of his candidacy. Privately, she expressed concern for his safety. Her concern deepened to palpable fear on April 4, 1968, when Martin Luther King was murdered in Memphis. She wasn't just afraid for Bobby; she began to believe America was not a safe place to raise her children, who carried the Kennedy name.

On March 31, President Johnson announced he would not seek reelection. Instead, his vice president, Hubert Humphrey, also entered the race. Bobby quickly became the front-runner, although McCarthy stayed close behind, and even upset Bobby in the Oregon primary. It was the first time a Kennedy had lost a political race of any kind. But Bobby bounced back and won the all-important California primary. After making his victory speech at the Ambassador Hotel in Los Angeles, Kennedy and his entourage walked through the kitchen, where Sirhan Bishara Sirhan was waiting for him. Sirhan fired several shots, striking Bobby three times and wounding five others. Sirhan, a Palestinian, later stated he was angry over Kennedy's support of Israel.

Jackie was awakened at 4:00 A.M. by her brother-in-law, Stas Radziwill, who told her Bobby had been shot. Accompanied by two friends, Jackie left immediately on a private jet for Los Angeles. When she landed, Jackie was given the news: Although Bobby had survived the shooting and his heart was beating, he was brain dead and was on life support. He would not survive.

THEY SAID ...

"Jackie was the one who turned off the machines. She flew in and nobody else had the nerve. . . . Ethel was in no shape to do anything. . . . Teddy was kneeling in prayer at the foot of the bed and finally Jackie came in and told the doctors they had to do it. It was the final seal for her."

—Richard Goodwin, *America's Queen*

Once again, the nation watched a black-veiled Jackie mourning. Although she remained composed in public, the ordeal of going through another death devastated her. After Jack's death, at least Bobby had been there to lean on. Now he was gone, leaving a gaping void in her life. More than that, her fears had been proven true. The murders of Martin Luther King Jr. and now Bobby left Jackie terrified. She needed to find a way to ensure her children's safety. There was only one person who could give Jackie the security, both financial and physical, that she desperately needed. That person was Aristotle Onassis.

Chapter 14

THE GREEK TYCOON

To the media, it was a modern day "Beauty and the Beast." It seemed incomprehensible that someone as refined and tasteful as Jackie would marry a brash, uncouth man like Aristotle Onassis. But this was no passionate love affair. This was an amicable business arrangement that gave both exactly what they wanted at the time.

Aristotle Onassis

Aristotle Socrates Onassis was born on January 20, 1906, in Smyrna, Turkey, to Anatolian Greek parents. His father, Socrates, was a successful tobacco trader. Onassis and his sister, Artemis, grew up in wealth but were touched by tragedy early. Their mother died when Onassis was six years old.

> **FACT**
>
> Anatolia is the name of the peninsula that forms the Asian side of Turkey. The European side is called Thrace or Rumelia. Anatolia, which is also known as Asia Minor, comes from the Greek word for "east." The ancient city of Troy was located in Anatolia, and Onassis's hometown, Smyrna, was the reputed birthplace of Homer, author of the *Iliad* and the *Odyssey*.

After World War I, the area was briefly occupied by Greece. But when Turkey recaptured Smyrna, the Onassis family lost everything. Then, because the Onassis family was Christian, they were persecuted by the Islamic government. Several members of Onassis's family were put in prison and sent to work camps. Three of his uncles were executed by hanging. The family moved to Greece as impoverished refugees, leaving just before the Turkish Army conducted a massacre of non-Turkish citizens.

A year later, in 1923, Onassis sailed to Argentina, leaving home with just $63 in his pocket. He supported himself with a succession of odd jobs: dishwasher, telephone operator, construction worker. He eventually established a thriving tobacco business in Argentina. He moved to New York and used that nest egg to invest in shipping tankers. He was a millionaire by the time he was twenty-five.

Around 1940, Onassis moved to Hollywood, where he lived the life of a rich bachelor. He dated movie stars—including Joe Kennedy's former mistress, Gloria Swanson—and ingratiated himself to the entertainment community. But by 1946, he was ready to start a family. He returned to Greece and began wooing Athina

Livanos, the seventeen-year-old daughter of Greece's wealthiest shipping magnate, Stavros Livanos. It wasn't love that spurred Onassis's advances; it was partly business and partly revenge. Onassis bitterly resented Livanos and other members of the Greek shipping union for refusing to let him participate in a very lucrative deal with the U.S. government. By marrying Athina, Livanos had no choice but to accept Onassis, who many considered a shady businessman at best. When Tina's sister Eugenia married Stavros Niarchos, Onassis joined with his father-in-law and new brother-in-law to form the most powerful shipping group in the world.

Onassis kept looking for ways to expand his business empire. In 1953, he acquired a majority interest in SBM, which controlled much of Monaco. Through SBM Onassis co-owned one-third of Monaco's real estate. Next, Onassis tried to make an exclusive deal with the Saudis to transport their oil in his tankers. It was at this point that Onassis's business practices came under scrutiny from the U.S. government. The FBI investigated Onassis and discovered fraud—by law, all ships carrying the American flag must be owned by an American citizen. Onassis pled guilty and paid a $7 million fine. His run-in with U.S. authorities also cost Onassis the deal with the Saudis. Undaunted, three years later he founded Olympic Airlines, the national carrier of Greece.

When the Suez Canal closed in 1956, Onassis made millions because he was the only independent ship owner with enough available tankers to transport oil around Africa's Cape of Good Hope. It was around that time that Onassis first met Jackie Kennedy when she and John F. Kennedy went for drinks aboard Onassis's yacht, *Christina*.

FACT

Onassis invited the young senator and his wife on board the yacht to meet Sir Winston Churchill, one of John F. Kennedy's idols. While the meeting between Churchill and Kennedy was anticlimactic, Onassis was immediately taken with Jackie.

Onassis and Athina had two children—Alexander, born in 1948, and Christina, born in 1950—but the marriage was far from perfect. Onassis was a serial adulterer, and his wife could not ignore the infidelities. She became addicted to alcohol and painkillers. The marriage unraveled for good when Onassis began a very public affair with opera singer Maria Callas, and the couple divorced in 1960. By that time, Onassis was one of the richest men in the world.

Onassis and Callas

Maria Callas was born in 1923 in the United States to Greek immigrant parents. When their marriage broke up, thirteen-year-old Maria left school and went to Athens, where her mother pushed her into singing. She established herself as a singer when she went to Italy and met Giovanni Battista Meneghini, whom she later married despite the thirty-year age difference between them. Under his direction, Callas became an opera star and jet-set celebrity. But her notoriety would ultimately have as much to do with her personal life as her talent.

THEY SAID...

"My sister was slim and beautiful and friendly, and my mother always preferred her. I was the ugly duckling, fat and clumsy and unpopular.... I'll never forgive her for taking my childhood away. During all the years I should have been playing and growing up, I was singing or making money."

—Maria Callas, *Time* magazine

Onassis and Callas first met in 1957 while attending a masked ball in Venice. They were introduced by society gossip columnist Elsa Maxwell. Two years later, Ari invited the Churchills, Callas, and Meneghini on a three-week cruise through the Greek islands, embarking from Monaco. By the time the cruise ended, Callas and Onassis had fallen in love and were already in the midst of an affair, despite the presence of their spouses on board. Both marriages ended soon after. On March 30, 1960, Callas gave birth to a son, who died after just a few hours. It was a tragedy that would forever bond them.

FACT

Purchased in 1954, the *Christina* was considered the most luxurious private yacht in the world. Renovated for $4 million, it included teak wood decks, a dry-cleaning plant, 18 cabins, a lapis lazuli fireplace, and a full-size movie screen. The dance floor opened to reveal a pool. The yacht costs more than $1 million annually to maintain.

Callas and Onassis were not discreet. Their passionate, volatile romance was very public, and the couple constantly made headlines in newspaper gossip sections the world over. Despite their obvious devotion, there was no talk of marriage. Callas later claimed that she instinctively knew getting married would change the dynamic of the relationship. She also believed there would be different expectations in a marriage than there were in a love affair. Callas was never blinded by love. She was keenly aware of Onassis's faults and his desire to conquer and acquire beyond financial wealth. Nor would she swear to his honesty in business. But his decision to marry Jackie Kennedy completely blind-sided Callas, who had long been aware of Onassis's fascination with her.

Fateful Cruise

Aristotle Onassis had met Jackie on several occasions during her marriage to Jack. After Patrick's death in August 1963, she had accepted an invitation from him to cruise the Mediterranean on his yacht with her sister and other guests. On that occasion, some suspected Onassis was simply trying to develop a relationship with the Kennedys that could help him get some contracts with the U.S.

government, something he hadn't been able to do since being found guilty of fraud by the FBI. But it was obvious to others that he also found Jackie beguiling.

THEY SAID...

"There's something damned willful about her; there's something provocative about that lady. She's got a carnal soul."

—Aristotle Onassis, *Ari: The Life and Times of Aristotle Socrates Onassis*

Beginnings of a Relationship

The route the cruise took, from Smyrna to Ithaca, was intended to impress the guests. It was also symbolic of how Onassis saw himself: as a modern-day Odysseus who overcame many obstacles on his journey to success. Jackie, for one, was intrigued by Onassis's colorful past. Not everyone in her husband's administration, however, shared her fascination. Some of his advisors were worried that having the First Lady socializing with a man of questionable business ethics might be a political liability—especially with the election a little over a year away. Kennedy defended his wife's desire to go on the trip. Even so, the White House issued a statement saying the First Lady was going to leave on a vacation to Greece with her sister and brother-in-law, carefully omitting any mention of Onassis.

For the first few days, Onassis was scarcely around, spending most of his time alone in his room. At Jackie's urging, he became more social, and she listened to his stories until late into the night. She asked him flirtatious questions, which he answered coyly. There has been speculation that Jackie and Onassis became physically intimate on the cruise. Friends adamantly deny she would have risked the reputation of the presidency to get involved with anyone while she was First Lady. But there's no dispute that by the time the cruise ended, there was a mutual, if tacit, attraction between the two. Jackie had always been drawn to wealthy, powerful men; Onassis enjoyed the added clout having a direct line to the Kennedys gave him. Each of Onassis's guests received a gift at the end of the trip. Jackie's was a gold and ruby bracelet worth nearly a half a million dollars in today's currency. It was the first move in a long-term seduction.

SHE SAID . . .

"I picked up the newspaper today, and read this story about this absolutely horrible woman—and it was me. I just don't understand sometimes why they work so hard at hurting me. There are so many more important things to do."

Secret Liaisons

Jackie moved to New York after Kennedy's death, and Onassis—who owned a suite at the Pierre Hotel—became a regular fixture in Jackie's life. They met for dinner in Manhattan and Paris, and he attended dinner parties she threw. Neither the media nor most of Jackie's circle imagined that she was romantically involved with Onassis, so few paid attention to their ongoing relationship, especially since Onassis was still involved with Callas.

By early 1968, Jackie had begun to seriously contemplate marrying Onassis. Bobby and most of the other Kennedys were not supportive and asked her to delay any decision until after the election. They also worried that Jackie's relationship with Onassis would sully the Kennedy name. Jackie's sister was equally unhappy but for different reasons. Lee had allegedly had an affair with Onassis previously and had wanted to marry him, but Onassis was not interested in marrying Lee. So when he started pursuing Jackie, it was a double blow to her. Many people point to this rebuff as the root of Lee and Jackie's eventual estrangement.

Jackie's Quest for Security

Bobby Kennedy's assassination convinced Jackie that the Kennedys were being targeted for their political and ideological beliefs. She became increasingly concerned for her children's safety and her own. Beyond their physical safety she also worried about their emotional development—the constant attention from the public and media in every aspect of their lives had became unrelenting and oppressive.

Jackie's solution was to marry Onassis. He could provide Jackie with financial freedom and make her less beholden to the Kennedys. Although she would have to give up her Secret Service detail, Jackie knew Onassis had the wealth—estimated at half a billion dollars—and the power to keep her family safe. Onassis could also ensure a certain measure of privacy. In turn, Onassis thought marrying Jackie would get him the respectability he craved. So he broke off his nine-year affair with Maria Callas and presented Jackie with a 40-carat engagement ring.

In September 1968, Jackie took Onassis to visit Rose Kennedy. Jackie wanted Rose's blessing. Although she would have gone ahead with her plans regardless, she wanted the mother of her husband to understand that marrying Onassis in no way diminished Jack's memory, nor could it replace him in her heart. Rose had known Onassis socially for several years and found him articulate, amusing, and charismatic. Still, she had concerns about their age difference, about the religious differences, and about how Caroline and John Jr. would adjust to having Onassis as a stepfather. But Rose also knew Jackie was not a person who jumped rashly into anything important.

On October 20, 1968, less than five months after Bobby Kennedy's assassination, Jackie Kennedy married Aristotle Onassis. The Greek Orthodox ceremony was held on Onassis's private Aegean island, Skorpios. Jackie had kept her plans so secret that her mother almost didn't make the ceremony—Janet couldn't find her passport and was only able to travel after the State Department gave her a special clearance. When news of their marriage became public, there was an outcry the world over. Newspaper headlines from the United States to Europe expressed shock and outrage. Some lamented that America had lost a saint; others described the pairing as sad and shameful. A report that her prenuptial agreement included a $5 million wedding gift added to the sense that Jackie had sold out her good name.

SHE SAID . . .

"She of all people was the one who encouraged me. She's been extraordinarily generous. I was married to her son and I have his children, but she was the one who was saying, if this is what you think is best, go ahead."

Contrary to popular belief, Jackie never moved her children to Greece. They continued attending private school in New York then spent a month and a half every summer on Skorpios. They also spent time at his home in Paris.

While Onassis made an effort to befriend Caroline and John, Jackie's relationship with his children was chilly. Both Alex and Christina had grown up largely ignored by their parents. Onassis was busy running his businesses and spending time with Callas while Athina filled her emptiness with parties, travel, and drugs. Instead of giving their time, they gave their children their every whim, and both Alex and Christina grew up into spoiled and demanding adults. Alex was openly hostile toward Jackie for taking his mother's place as Mrs. Onassis. Christina desperately wanted her father's approval and saw Jackie as an obstacle to his affection. However, Christina and Alex liked Caroline and John Jr., and the stepsiblings spent many happy times together during the summers.

Aristotle and Jackie Onassis celebrate their first anniversary, 1969

Photo Credit: Time & Life Pictures/Getty Images

Separate Lives

Gossip columns speculated endlessly about the Onassis relationship, but by all accounts of friends and family, the newlyweds appeared happy.

The Honeymoon

Jackie was so immersed in her new husband that Caroline and John Jr. were regularly left with Janet and the children's new governess, Marta Sgubin. In 1969, the *Christina* was based in Puerto Rico so Jackie would fly the children and Marta down on weekends to spend time with them or they would vacation in Palm Beach. But Jackie's favorite place was Skorpios. She rhapsodized about the color of the water and the fragrant flowers that grew everywhere. It was a sanctuary where she could fully relax and not worry about who might be watching her.

Even so, Jackie and Aristo, as she called him, never really lived under the same roof for any length of time. When he came to New York for business, he stayed at her 1040 apartment. Otherwise, he stayed at his Pierre Hotel suite for tax reasons. When she went to Skorpios for the summer, Onassis would be there for only a few days at a time before leaving on yet another business trip. And when he was on the island, he all but lived on the *Christina*. Jackie, who thought the yacht was pretentious, lived in one of the houses that she had redecorated with Onassis's blessing.

THEY SAID...

"Jackie loves traveling, sightseeing, long walks, mountain climbing, skiing, and literally hundreds of things that are just not to my liking. . . . I know Jackie would eventually give up her activities to please me and just stay with me, but then, that wouldn't really be Jackie. I didn't want that to happen."

—Aristotle Onassis

The Turning Point

In February 1970, it was reported that four letters Jackie had written to Ros Gilpatrick would be put up for auction by a Washington, D.C., gallery. Gilpatrick, who had been President Kennedy's Deputy Secretary of Defense, had been Jackie's constant companion in the summer of 1968. Their trip together to the Yucatan peninsula had been widely reported in the press. But whether their relationship had been platonic or romantic was a matter of conjecture among her friends.

How the gallery came by the letters was not revealed, although the same day the announcement was made, Gilpatrick's wife filed for divorce and insinuated in an interview with the *Chicago Daily News* that her husband's relationship with Jackie had been more than simple friendship. The inference sent shockwaves through Jackie's inner circle. Nancy Tuckerman issued a statement denying that Jackie had in any way been involved in the breakup of the Gilpatricks' marriage.

Onassis knew that Jackie and Gilpatrick had been close, so that did not concern him. However, the fact that one of the letters had been written while Jackie and Onassis were on their honeymoon infuriated Onassis. Not only was he insulted that Jackie was writing warm, flirty notes to another man on her honeymoon, the fact that it was now public made Onassis feel like a fool.

THEY SAID...

"He was not in love with Jackie. And in his own opinion, he never protested that he was—she was an acquisition. She was a trophy wife. Jackie was the biggest trophy in the world and he was going to have her."

—Peter Evans, *Entertainment Tonight*

A few months later, Onassis spent four days with Callas, and photographs of them together appeared in the press. It was the first public indication that Onassis had resumed his relationship with the opera singer. Although it did not have an immediate impact on their marriage, it was clear the honeymoon was definitely over.

Soul Mate

For all the affection and attraction Onassis had for Jackie, Callas remained his soul mate. They shared the same heritage and, in many ways, the same volatile temperament. Their arguments were epic, but Callas always stayed and fought it out until the anger was depleted. Jackie's style was to say nothing and leave the room, leaving Onassis frustrated. As the marriage wore on, Onassis became increasingly restless. Their long-distance marriage quickly evolved into a marriage of separate lives.

Jackie spent more and more time in New York with her children. She also spent more time shopping. She and Onassis argued over her prodigious spending, prompting him to once ask if there was a twelve-step program for shopaholics. Because Onassis knew most people assumed she had simply married him for his money, he felt her prolific spending made him look like a patsy. But Jackie was not cowed by Onassis's rages.

SHE SAID . . .

"I am a very shy person. Some people take this for arrogance, and my withdrawal from publicity as a sign of my supposedly looking down at the rest of mankind."

He told friends that inside her demure white gloves were fists of rock. Despite the strain, there was no public indication that either of them wanted out of the marriage.

Jackie and the Media

From the time she married Jack, Jackie had been a fixture in the news media. Sometimes, such as when magazines dwelt on her wardrobe, she found the coverage silly. Other times she found it intrusive, but it was never mean-spirited. There was always an undercurrent of respect for Jackie as an individual. That was especially true after Kennedy's assassination. But after Jackie married Aristotle Onassis, her relationship with the media changed. No longer a Kennedy in the public's eye, the press dubbed her "Jackie O."

The Original "Tabloid Queen"

It could be argued that the *National Enquirer* changed the face of American journalism. Its blend of inspirational human interest features and sensational coverage of celebrities struck a chord with readers hungry to learn that the rich and famous really weren't that much different from themselves. The *Enquirer* treated gossip seriously and unapologetically.

In 1969, the *Enquirer*'s publisher, Generoso Pope, ran an article on Jackie Onassis. The highly unflattering piece was based on an interview with Caroline and John's former nanny. Sales of the

Enquirer jumped significantly. While Americans may not have been enamored with Jackie as much since her marriage to Onassis, they were still intrigued by her.

After that issue, Gene Pope put Jackie on the cover of the *Enquirer* every chance he got. Whether the story was genuine and newsworthy, superficial, or basically fiction, Jackie was the new tabloid queen. Pope would have freelancers create stories around paparazzi photographs of Jackie. It was the *Enquirer* that ran the expose on Jackie's aunt, Edith Bouvier, living in squalor in her East Hampton mansion. The article prompted the Suffolk County New York Board of Health to raid the home and cite Edith, ordering her to clean up the premises.

Galella v. Onassis

Considered one of America's first true paparazzi, photojournalist Ron Galella developed the innovative technique of catching his subjects by surprise to catch their reactions or by following them going about their daily lives and taking their pictures in everyday settings.

Jackie Onassis and Ron Galella in New York City, 1971

Photo Credit: Ron Galella/ WireImage

Galella was particularly relentless when it came to Jackie, stalking her on basically a daily basis. He took literally thousands of pictures of Jackie over a period of fifteen years. He interrupted Caroline's tennis lessons to get shots of her, bribed people to reveal Jackie's whereabouts, showed up in a powerboat where Jackie was swimming, and generally stalked the family relentlessly. But when Galella used his "jump out and surprise" tactic on John Jr., it set off a lawsuit that would pit a celebrity's right to privacy against a photographer's First Amendment protections.

In October 1969, Ron Galella encountered Jackie and John Jr. as they returned home from a bike ride in Central Park. He was able to take several pictures before Jackie saw him. According to Galella, she ordered John's Secret Service guards to apprehend him and break the camera. He alleged he was driven to a police station and given the choice of giving up the film or getting arrested. He kept the film and was subsequently charged with harassment.

After his acquittal, Galella sued Onassis, charging he was falsely arrested and maliciously prosecuted. His lawyer also claimed Galella was

SHE SAID . . .

"Aristotle Onassis rescued me at a moment when my life was engulfed with shadows. He brought me into a world where one could find both happiness and love. We lived through many beautiful experiences together which cannot be forgotten, and for which I will be eternally grateful."

protected by the First Amendment to photograph Onassis in public. Jackie countersued for damages and injunctive relief against Galella, saying she lived in dread fear of the photographer. In the end, the court dismissed Galella's claims and granted Jackie injunctive relief, requiring Galella to stay at least fifty yards away from her and one hundred yards away from her apartment building. That was later reduced to twenty-five feet.

FACT

In the course of his career, Galella angered more than one celebrity. In June 1973, Marlon Brando broke his jaw and knocked out four of his teeth. Brigitte Bardot once had him hosed down. While trying to photograph Richard Burton and Elizabeth Taylor in Mexico, Galella was beaten up by Burton's bodyguards.

In 1982, Jackie brought another suit against Galella, claiming he had violated terms of the injunction on at least a dozen occasions. Rather than risk huge fines and jail time if found guilty, Galella agreed to never photograph Jackie again. Ironically, after Jackie's death, John Kennedy Jr. reached out to Galella, and the photographer chronicled John Jr.'s life until his tragic plane crash.

Aristotle's Death

Onassis contacted infamous lawyer Roy Cohn to discuss his options for divorce. Because he had assets in the United States as well as Greece, he needed American representation. But the discussions were cut short.

On January 22, 1973, the plane Alexander Onassis was piloting crashed on takeoff. He suffered severe head trauma and irreversible brain damage and died the next day. Onassis was inconsolable and never fully recovered from his grief. Although he still intended to divorce Jackie, his health failed him first.

Jackie was in New York when she got a phone call from Christina that Aristotle had collapsed with severe abdominal pains. Christina also called prominent New York heart specialist Isadore Rosenfeld, who flew to Athens with Jackie. At the hospital, Rosenfeld and Jean Caroli, a gastroenterologist from Paris, met to discuss Onassis's condition. The two specialists deeply disagreed on how to best treat Onassis. Caroli wanted him transported to the American Hospital in Paris to have his gall bladder removed. Rosenfeld believed Onassis was far too weak to undergo surgery but should fly to New York for treatment. Christina made the decision to let Caroli perform the surgery.

Onassis was so weak his butler had to carry him to the car as they left for Paris. His gall bladder was removed on February 10. His condition immediately worsened, and he was placed on life support. Although it was clear he was dying, doctors told Jackie it would not be a quick passing. During his time in the hospital, Jackie commuted between Paris and New York, where her children were. In March, she flew back to New York to host a small dinner party on the night an NBC documentary that Caroline had worked on was airing.

FACT

The American Hospital of Paris was founded in 1906. It is a private, not-for-profit hospital that is equipped with state-of-the-art diagnostic equipment. The medical staff includes more than 500 physicians and surgeons. It is also the only civilian hospital in Europe accredited by America's Joint Commission on Accreditation of Healthcare Organizations, known for its rigorous standards.

Christina never left her father's side, nor did she want to share him in his final hours. When Onassis was finally near death, she instructed the doctors not to inform anyone. It was Onassis's sister, Artemis, who called Jackie and told her to hurry back to Paris. But as she was packing to leave the following morning, on March 15, Artemis called to say Onassis had died. Only Christina had been at his bedside.

Jackie Onassis with her children at Aristotle Onassis's funeral, 1975

Photo Credit: Keystone/Hulton Archive/Getty Images

In the aftermath of Aristotle's death, Jackie came under intense criticism in the Greek media for being in New York when her husband died. Her lack of tears during the funeral further ostracized her from the Greek public. However, she promised Christina that she would keep the Onassis name permanently.

THEY SAID...

"Once I was visiting Jackie in her New York apartment, after Ari Onassis died. . . . Christina unexpectedly dropped in. Jackie and Christina sat there, telling stories about Ari and laughing together. They certainly were not fighting."

—Mark Riboud, in *As We Remember Her*

In April, the *New York Times* published a story about Ari's intention to divorce Jackie. The article also discussed Christina's bitterness toward her former stepmother. The story upset Jackie so much she called Christina and asked her to deny it, which she did. But the negotiation between the lawyers for Jackie's financial settlement was tense and drawn-out.

Christina claimed there was no will and initially offered Jackie a couple million dollars. After the two agreed to $20 million, Onassis's will surfaced. According to the terms of the handwritten will, Christina inherited 55 percent of her father's estate. The other 45 percent went to fund the Alexander S. Onassis Foundation. Jackie's attorneys threatened legal action, claiming that Christina had intentionally misrepresented herself. The final settlement was reached in September 1977. In addition to the $20 million, Jackie would receive $200,000 a year for the rest of her life. Caroline and John would get $25,000 a year until they reached the age of twenty-one. All payments were to be adjusted for inflation. In exchange, Jackie agreed to give up her share of Skorpios, Ari's yacht, and her position on the board of the Onassis Foundation.

Chapter 15

LITERATI

After Aristotle's death, Jackie returned to New York financially secure and ready to put down roots. Her jet-setting days over, she settled into a comfortable existence, balancing the vibrancy of the city with the serenity of her country home. She also went back to work, this time not as a writer but as an editor, which allowed her to immerse herself in the arts on a more personal level.

Jackie's New York

Before his death, Aristotle bought Jackie a $200,000 estate in Bernardsville, New Jersey. It was a two-frame house on ten acres of hunt country that was her special refuge—a place to ride, to write, to recharge. In Martha's Vineyard, Jackie built a nineteen-room summerhouse on 375 acres of ocean-front land. When she was in New York City, she continued to live at her Fifth Avenue apartment, using Central Park as her personal backyard. Even before Onassis's death, Jackie had become increasingly involved in preserving the city's history. Jackie wrote a review of the International Center for Photography for the *New Yorker* as an anonymous essay titled "Being Present."

Fight for Grand Central Station

A week after the *New Yorker* article was published, Jackie became publicly involved in the fight to save Grand Central Terminal. The Landmarks Preservation Commission had named it a historical landmark, but Penn Central, which owned Grand Central, claimed it was in dire financial straits and wanted to sell the property to a developer who was threatening to build a fifty-five story office building on the site. In order for the deal to go through, the landmark status would have to be overruled, and a judge did so on January 21, 1975. When Jackie heard about the ruling, she joined the fight to save Grand Central.

Her first call was to Kent Barwick, who was the director of the Municipal Art Society. She told him she wanted to help and offered to volunteer. That was the beginning of her long association with the MAS. When the society held a lighting ceremony to draw attention to its efforts to save

SHE SAID . . .

"A big corporation shouldn't be able to destroy a building that has meant so much to so many for so many generations. If Grand Central Station goes, all of the landmarks in this country will go as well. If that happens, we'll live in a world of steel and glass. This is . . . an issue that represents all issues."

the station, it was Jackie who pulled the switch—and catapulted the story to the front page of the next day's *New York Times.*

The fight to save Grand Central moved to the courts. The New York Supreme Court ruled that the building's landmark designation prevented Penn Central from selling it for development. But a federal appellate court overruled the state court. It would come down to a matter of public opinion. Jackie became a tireless advocate, appearing at rallies to drum up support. When the MAS was in Washington, D.C., to appeal the appellate ruling before the Supreme Court, Jackie led a delegation by train to the nation's capital. At each stop, local officials met the train in order to meet Jackie.

The publicity generated by the train trip and a subsequent press conference brought the fight for Grand Central onto the front pages of newspapers across the country. Jackie made the issue relevant to people from around the country, not only New Yorkers. People wrote letters to their congressional representatives, and donations poured into the MAS.

Ultimately, the Supreme Court upheld the landmark status, noting that the public's interest factored into its decision. Today, there is a plaque inside Grand Central that acknowledges Jackie's role in saving it.

New York City Programs

Jackie was involved in other preservation groups, including the Citizens Committee for New York City, which was created in 1975 to help New Yorkers confront problems the nearly bankrupt city could not deal with itself.

Jackie also joined the board of the Forty-Second Street Development Corporation, which was established to revitalize the Times Square area. Jackie was able to get the mayor's office to cooperate, and her participation generated media interest. Jackie knew her participation with any group would generate public interest, so she picked her causes carefully. When she joined a cause, it was more than just in name. Jackie attended meetings, made phone calls, and helped raise money and awareness.

A New Career

In 1950, Jackie had met a writer working for the *Paris Review* named Tom Guinzburg. Twenty-five years later, he was president of Viking Press. Guinzburg offered Jackie a job as an editor, in part because of her love and knowledge of literature, and partly because of her wealth of contacts. Jackie accepted and started work in September 1975, earning $10,000 a year and working four days a week. Her coworkers found her to be down-to-earth and accessible. Jackie immersed herself into the work, finding it intellectually stimulating and creatively fulfilling.

Viking Press editors Bryan Holme and Jackie Onassis look over their book, *In the Russian Style,* 1977

Photo Credit: Alfred Eisenstaedt/ Time & Life Pictures/Getty Images

A Controversy

Two years later, one of Viking's authors, Jeffrey Archer, wrote a thriller called *Shall We Tell the President*. The plot was about an assassination of a future president—namely Ted Kennedy. According to Guinzburg, he told Jackie about the book. He claimed that Jackie gave her blessing, saying as long as she didn't have to read it she wouldn't object to Viking publishing the book. But Jackie told friends Guinzburg had never told her what the plot was about other than it was about Ted Kennedy. She trusted Tom and thought no more about it.

> **FACT**
> Before becoming a successful author, Jeffrey Archer was a British politician. He was a member of parliament and deputy chairman of the Conservative Party. But his political career came to an abrupt end after he was convicted of perjury in relation to an insider trading investigation. After serving his prison term, Archer started writing.

When the book came out, it caused an uproar. The *New York Times* gave the book a scathing review and took a shot at Jackie, saying she should be ashamed of herself for working at a publisher that would print such a book. Jackie was barraged with calls from Kennedys. She told everyone she didn't know anything about what was in the book, which was true since she hadn't read it. In an interview with the *Boston Globe*, Guinzburg maintained Jackie had known about the book all along.

Jackie was so upset and angry that she quit, refusing to see or even talk to Guinzburg. She sent him a handwritten resignation letter via messenger, and their friendship was irrevocably ruined. A short time later, Guinzburg was fired, in part because of the Archer debacle.

Doubleday

In 1978, Jackie was hired as an associate editor at Doubleday by another old friend, John Sargent. Her former social secretary and best friend, Nancy Tuckerman, also worked at Doubleday, and the two women worked closely together for the next fifteen years. Just as she had been at Viking, Jackie was well liked and respected. She did not get, or want, preferential treatment, pitching her ideas along with everyone else at editorial meetings.

Because she didn't need to build a contact list, Jackie seldom participated in the publishing social scene. She frequently ate lunch at her desk instead of going to mingle with the lunchtime publishing crowd at high-profile restaurants. The job accommodated her lifestyle: Jackie worked just three days a week and spent summers on Martha's Vineyard.

THEY SAID...

"She was not just accessible, she was genuinely caring. She also had a wicked sense of humor and was a lot of fun. She really connected with the authors, too, once they got over the idea that their editor was Jackie Kennedy Onassis. She was warm, engaging, smart—a friend."

—Stephen Rubin, president and publisher of Doubleday

Jackie's Authors

On average, Jackie edited ten to twelve books a year. Her titles were primarily nonfiction, with an emphasis on history and the performing arts, especially ballet and music. Her eclectic tastes were reflected in the books she oversaw, including Bill Moyers's *Healing and the Mind*, Michael Jackson's *Moonwalk*, and Edvard Radzinsky's *The Last Tsar: The Life and Death of Nicholas II*. She published a number of children's books by singer Carly Simon, who was a neighbor on Martha's Vineyard. Her passion for Egypt prompted her to acquire and publish the translation for the Cairo Trilogy—*Palace*

Walk, Palace of Desire, and *Sugar Street*—by Nobel Prize–winning Egyptian author Naguib Mahfouz.

Working with Jackie

Jackie gave her authors much more one-on-one time and attention than a typical editor. She would conduct editing sessions either at her office or at 1040. Since she chose books that reflected her interests, she was passionate about each project and very knowledgeable. Jackie was also considerate and made sure not to hurt an author's feelings if she had a negative criticism to make. All her authors spoke of Jackie's attention to detail and her bottomless curiosity. She had found a career that was perfectly suited to her both intellectually and emotionally.

In April 1993 Jackie agreed to an interview with *Publishers Weekly* editorial director John F. Baker—as long as their conversation was not tape recorded or photographed and there would be no questions about her personal life. She also received copy approval.

The interview was arranged at the suggestion of Doubleday president Stephen Rubin. Jackie was just happy to talk about her work and explained to Baker that being an editor was a natural fit—she majored in literature in college, had many friends who were writers, and, most importantly, loved books. Plus, in publishing it was the author and the book who were promoted—not the editor. Baker sent Jackie a copy of the article, and Jackie only made two changes: one to correct a name and the other to correct his grammar.

THEY SAID...

"One would not associate her with a book of articles from *Rolling Stone* or a comic book history of the universe. . . . She is extraordinarily devoted to the books she has edited, especially the looks, the esthetic appeal. Her greatest enthusiasm is devoted to finding the books and making sure they are designed and produced as elegantly and pleasingly as possible. . . ."

—John F. Baker

❝SHE SAID . . .

"In the city parks we feel Atget's humanity. He photographs with tenderness and melancholy. In the Tuileries, the park chair, as French as the croissant, lies overturned beside a leering faun . . . we find these photographs troubling because we connect to them. . . . Our grandfathers sit in black serge suits along the paths laid out by kings and queens."

Jackie's involvement and support surprised many of her authors. Canadian writer Robertson Davies recalled the time he was being honored at an American university. He looked out from the podium and was stunned to see Jackie mingling in the crowd. Jackie was particularly interested in showcasing the contributions of African American writers. She encouraged another Martha's Vineyard neighbor, Dorothy West, to work on what eventually became *The Wedding*. West, the last surviving member of the Harlem Renaissance, published the book in 1995, and three years later Oprah Winfrey adapted it into a television movie starring Halle Berry.

The New York Publishing Scene

New York has long been the literary center of America. It is the home of numerous professional organizations, institutions, and journals, including the PEN American Center, *The New York Review of Books*, and *New York Quarterly*. The city has also been home to a Who's Who of American writers through the centuries, from Dorothy Parker and Thomas Pynchon to Norman Mailer and Don DeLillo.

FACT

Washington Irving enjoyed popularity and critical respect in Europe after writing *History of New York* in 1809. The Victorian era satire's protagonist is a quintessential Dutch New Yorker named Diedrich Knickerbocker. It was from that character that the term *knickerbocker*, meaning old-fashioned Dutch-descended New Yorker, became part of the lexicon—and the name for New York's professional basketball team, affectionately known as the Knicks.

Harlem Renaissance

One of the most important literary movements in New York was the Harlem Renaissance, which established the African American literary canon in the United States. During its peak in the years leading up to the Great Depression, Harlem attracted not just black American writers migrating north but immigrant authors from Africa and the Caribbean. Harlem authors wrote books and essays that challenged the racism that remained pervasive in American society. There was no single style that defined the Harlem Renaissance; it was more a spirit of self-expression and independence.

THEY SAID...

"What happens to a dream deferred?
Does it dry up
like a raisin in the sun?
Or fester like a sore—
And then run?
Does it stink like rotten meat?
Or crust and sugar over—
like a syrupy sweet?
Maybe it just sags
like a heavy load.
Or does it explode?"

—Langston Hughes, *A Dream Deferred*

New York Intellectuals

The New York Intellectuals emerged in the mid-twentieth century, embracing left wing, anti-Stalinist political ideas. Their writing was characterized by an effort to integrate literary theory with Marxism. Many of the New York Intellectuals had attended City College of New York in the 1930s. Some had written for or edited the left-wing political journal *The Partisan Review*. Among the authors considered Intellectuals were Mary McCarthy, Robert Warshow, Lionel Trilling, and Sidney Hook.

Nuyorican Movement

New York has also been a fertile ground for Jewish American literature and the literature of other ethnic groups, including Nuyoricans, a term used to describe Puerto Ricans or their descendants who live in the New York City metropolitan area. Numbering an estimated 800,000, it is the largest Puerto Rican population outside of Puerto Rico.

FACT

Puerto Rican immigrants began arriving in New York in significant numbers during the 1930s. After World War II U.S. companies sent recruiters to Puerto Rico in search of cheap labor. Hundreds of thousands of Puerto Ricans left the island for New York. When the Great Migration ended in 1960, almost 10 percent of New York's population was Puerto Rican.

The Nuyorican Poets Café was the gathering spot where writers, musicians, and artists met to exchange ideas. The café originally began in 1973 as a get-together in the East Village apartment of poet Miguel Algarín. A college professor, Algarín was committed to promoting new artists. By 1975, the gathering, filled with Nuyorican poets, had grown too large for the professor's living room. Believing poetry needed to be read, and heard, Algarín rented an Irish bar called the Sunshine Cafe on East Sixth Street and renamed it the Nuyorican Poets Café. Today it remains one of the country's most highly respected arts organizations.

Other Literary Interests

Jackie showed her support for literature through avenues beyond editing. One of her close friends, photographer Peter Beard, had compiled a book of African folk tales. The book was illustrated with his photographs and those of writer Isak Dinesen, the pen name of Baroness Karen Blixen. The text of the book was by Blixen's cook, Kamante Gatura. Jackie read the manuscript, *Longing for Darkness*, and loved it so much she asked to write the forward. Her friendship with Beard rekindled Jackie's interest in photography. As an editor, she became especially noted for her work on photography books.

When the International Center of Photography announced an exhibit of French garden photos by Eugene Atget, who died in 1927, Jackie proposed a companion book, which reintroduced the otherwise forgotten photographer to both the general public and the photography community.

Her interest in photography was also personal. Although she shied away from high-tech cameras, she still took pictures with a simple camera and kept them in scrapbooks filled with personal photos of family and friends and her current horse, named Frank.

Kennedy Library and Museum

In 1975, plans to build the Kennedy Library at Harbor Point in Boston's Dorchester neighborhood finally moved forward. Jackie was involved with every detail. She was instrumental in selecting architect I. M. Pei to design the building. For the landscaping, she chose dune grass, commenting that Jack had always been a wind man. Jackie also made sure no unflattering photographs from the library's extensive collection were ever released. The library opened in 1979 and was officially dedicated in 1980.

Just as she did with the books she edited, Jackie willingly appeared at functions promoting the library, aware that her presence still generated publicity. After Ernest Hemingway's papers were donated to the Kennedy Library—the result of Jackie's personal efforts—she had a research room built for them.

Social Causes

The Bedford-Stuyvesant Project gave Jackie the opportunity to combine social awareness with artistic creativity. The project's goal was to build quality, affordable homes for low-income families in the economically challenged Bedford-Stuyvesant area of Brooklyn. She believed that African culture could inspire black-owned businesses in America. She paired some investors with local talent who created cloth designs inspired by Africa. Jackie then organized an exhibit of their work at the Metropolitan Museum of Art. To further promote the project, she invited selected photographers to come to 1040 and photograph the designs she had used in her own apartment as tablecloths and napkins. It was the first and last time she agreed to have her home photographed.

Jackie also supported the Coalition for the Homeless in Los Angeles, which assisted low-income youths. She spent time in the city's most economically depressed areas, talking to parents and teens, knowing that as always, her presence would generate much-needed publicity and exposure to the cause. In addition to giving her time, Jackie was a generous financial contributor to causes, both social and political. While her money gave her security and the freedom to help others, it was her children and the man who became her constant companion that truly completed Jackie.

Chapter 16

FAMILY TIES

As much as Jackie enjoyed her work and was fulfilled by her causes, family remained the most important thing in her life. Even though she would never marry again, Jackie did find a romantic partner who complemented her and offered her the companionship and intellectual challenge she needed.

Maurice Tempelsman

Not long after receiving her settlement from Christina Onassis, Jackie was seen with a new companion. His name was Maurice Tempelsman, and although friends initially insisted that Tempelsman was giving Jackie financial advice, it soon became apparent they were a couple. They had originally met when Jack was still a senator and Tempelsman was a Democratic supporter and a contributor to Kennedy's presidential campaign. His business acumen is also credited with helping Jackie turn her $26 million settlement into a fortune worth more than $100 million.

Jackie Kennedy Onassis and Maurice Tempelsman, 1990

Photo Credit: Brian Quigley/Time & Life Pictures/Getty Images

In the months following Aristotle Onassis's death, Tempelsman became Jackie's constant companion. To the general public, they seemed an odd couple—she was sleek and sophisticated, the epitome of New York high society. He was pudgy and unassuming. But Tempelsman was a successful, cultured man who collected art, was fluent in French, and exuded personal warmth. His social politics were similar to Jackie's—he supported African democratization and helped underwrite Nelson Mandela's first trip to the United States. However, his profession also added a hint of intrigue—and in some cases, suspicion.

FACT

Tempelsman was born in Antwerp, Belgium. His family were Orthodox Jews and fled Europe in 1940, just before the Nazis invaded Belgium. They moved to a refugee neighborhood in New York City, where Tempelsman's father founded a diamond broker-age. Tempelsman married Lily Bucholz, a teenage Polish Jewish refugee, in the late 1940s. They had three children together.

In 1990 the *Washington Post* reported that former California Democratic assemblyman Mervyn Dymally changed his position on diamond imports after a 1988 meeting with Tempelsman—and after Tempelsman contributed $34,200 to a Dymally-supported scholarship fund for minority students. The politician denied solic-iting the contribution or being influenced by it. Tempelsman also maintained the contribution was coincidental to Dymally's change of position.

Into the early 1980s, Tempelsman continued to describe himself as simply a family friend of Jackie's. But their demeanor was that of a couple. Gossip columns and newspapers were uncharacteristically muted about Jackie and Maurice. Jackie's children also accepted Tempelsman and shared a mutual affection with him.

In 1984, Tempelsman and his wife obtained the equivalent of an annulment for Orthodox Jews in 1984 but never legally or civ-illy divorced. In 1988, Tempelsman moved into Jackie's 1040 Fifth Avenue apartment.

THEY SAID...

"You know from what he says, as well as what he doesn't say, that there's a lively and fertile mind operating there. This is a world citizen we're talking about, at home in almost any culture he finds himself in."

—Chester Crocker, former U.S. assistant secretary of state for African affairs

Family Relationships

Throughout the most hectic and unsettled times of her life, Caroline and John were always Jackie's top priority. When Caroline was little, Jackie made sure they had time to read, play games, draw, and paint together. When she got older, they rode together.

Jackie and her children ride together, 1962

Photo Credit: John F. Kennedy Presidential Library and Museum, Boston

After the assassination, Jackie worked furiously to protect her children's privacy and create a safe haven for them to grow up away from public scrutiny. Being a Kennedy meant that some exposure was inevitable, but for the most part, Caroline and John grew up in a stable, protected environment. On most evenings Jackie ate dinner at home with her children. At Red Gate Farm, her Martha's Vineyard estate, she would kayak with John on Squibnocket Pond. Mindful of notoriety, Jackie always asked her children before attending one of their school functions. Once the other parents got over their initial surprise at seeing Jackie among them, she became just another proud parent.

THEY SAID...

"Her love for Caroline and John was deep and unqualified. She reveled in their accomplishments, she hurt with their sorrows. At the mere mention of one of their names, Jackie's eyes would shine brighter and her smile would grow bigger."

—Senator Ted Kennedy

While Jackie wanted to protect her children, she also wanted them to appreciate and respect the past; specifically the Kennedy and Bouvier histories. At the same time, she wanted them to think of themselves as distinct individuals, not just one of the Kennedy cousins. When John was twelve he participated in an Outward Bound program in Maine. When he was fifteen, John went to Guatemala with his cousin Timothy Shriver to help earthquake victims. The summer before starting college, John spent two months in the Peace Corps—an organization started by his father shortly after he became president. As he grew older, Jackie confided to friends that she anticipated John entering politics one day. She would support that decision but made sure that he had a solid educational foundation for such a venture.

Caroline and John

Although Jackie traveled frequently when her children were young, she gave them undivided time and attention when she was home. Jackie was their biggest cheerleader and also their most pointed critic. She was more than their mother—she was their touchstone. By the time they left the safety net of their childhood to start their own lives, they were thoughtful, well-adjusted young adults.

Caroline Kennedy

In 1975, Caroline graduated from Concord Academy. Instead of enrolling at Radcliffe right away, she decided to study abroad for a year first. Jackie gave her blessing, knowing how important her own time in Europe had been to her personal development. Like her mother, Caroline initially wanted to spend a year in Paris, but after learning about an art history program at Sotheby's in London, Caroline went to England instead.

It was arranged that she would stay with Hugh Fraser and his daughters, who were near Caroline's age. Fraser, recently divorced from author Antonia Fraser, was a Member of Parliament. Unbeknownst to Jackie, Fraser was on an IRA hit list for his views on Irish independence. In October 1975, the IRA detonated a bomb outside Fraser's Westminster home, killing a neighbor. Had it gone off five minutes later, Fraser would have been getting into his car to drive Caroline to the subway station. Jackie immediately moved Caroline in with her aunt and uncle, the Radziwills.

Caroline turned eighteen that November. Although her classes were challenging, she still found time for a social life. She was photographed at several clubs with Mark Shand, who had broken up with his girlfriend to be with Caroline. Shand's sister was Camilla Parker Bowles, who

> ## SHE SAID . . .
>
> "I'm going to bring up my son. I want him to grow up to be a good boy. I have no better dream for him. I want John to be a fine young man. He's so interested in planes; maybe he'll be an astronaut or just plain John Kennedy fixing planes on the ground."

would later divorce her husband and marry Prince Charles, so Shand's social contacts were extensive and he introduced Caroline to the cream of British society.

John F. Kennedy Jr.

Born less than three weeks after his father's election as president, John literally grew up in the public eye, known affectionately as John-John—a nickname his family never used. He got it when a White House reporter misunderstood what he heard Jack calling his son. What the president said was "John! . . . John!" He called his name twice, trying to get the boy's attention. What the reporter thought Jack said was John-John. The anecdote ran in the paper and the nickname stuck.

FACT

George was a glossy monthly magazine in the style of *Vanity Fair* that blended politics, lifestyle, and celebrity. Founded by John F. Kennedy Jr. and Michael Berman, it was published by Hachette Filipacchi. Its debut issue, which came out in September 1995, featured Cindy Crawford dressed as George Washington on the cover.

During the time his sister was in London, John attended Collegiate School. At fifteen he was maturing into a handsome youth, blessed with Black Jack's dark good looks and the Kennedy energy and athleticism. But academically he struggled with mediocre grades. He transferred to Phillips Academy for his junior and senior years and, despite his less than stellar grade point average, was accepted into Harvard, his father's alma mater and the school his sister Caroline was then attending. But John declined, not wanting to accept what was obvious preferential treatment based on family connections. Instead, he attended Brown University and majored in history. He graduated in 1983 and went on to study law. He failed the New York bar twice before finally passing in 1989. He worked in the Manhattan district attorney's office until leaving in 1993. Two years later he founded the magazine *George*.

6 SHE SAID . . .

"One must not dwell on only the tragedies that life holds for us all, just as a person must not just think of only the happiness and greatness that they've experienced. . . . Life is made up of both good and bad—and they cannot be separated from each other. It is a mistake to try and do that."

Although Jackie kept his life as private as possible, John always appeared at ease when confronted with the media. More intrusive was the security Jackie insisted on for her children. Friends say he was relieved when his Secret Service protection ended on his sixteenth birthday. From the moment he was of legal age, John was considered one of America's most eligible bachelors. Unlike his sister, who lived her life quietly behind the scenes, John was gregarious and social, frequently spotted coming out of New York's hottest nightclubs. He dated an assortment of A-list celebrities including Madonna, Sarah Jessica Parker, and Cindy Crawford and had a long relationship with actress Daryl Hannah.

Grand Jackie

With John content with playing the dating field, it fell to Caroline to fulfill Jackie's dream of becoming a grandmother. After graduating from Radcliffe, Caroline was hired as the manager and coordinating producer of the Metropolitan Museum of Art film and TV office. There, she met her future husband, Edwin Schlossberg. They were married in 1986 at Our Lady of Victory Roman Catholic Church on Cape Cod at Hyannis Port. Caroline was given away by her uncle, Ted Kennedy. Two years later, the couple's first child, Rose Kennedy Schlossberg, was born on June 25, 1988. Weighing in at seven pounds, twelve ounces, Rose was born at New York Hospital–Cornell Medical Center. A second daughter, Tatiana Celia Kennedy Schlossberg arrived May 5, 1990. Their third child, John Bouvier Kennedy Schlossberg was born on January 19, 1993.

Jackie doted on her grandchildren. When Rose began nursery school, Jackie was the only grandparent who accompanied the class on a field trip. Rose and her classmates walked down the block and across the street to explore Central Park. Jackie came dressed in jeans and tennis shoes and won over the other parents with her genuine interest in their children. Jackie once wrote Caroline a note calling her grandkids a wonderful gift that restored her faith in the family's future.

John Jr.'s Marriage

Jackie did not live to see it, but her son did eventually settle down. John Jr. wed Carolyn Bessette, a publicist for Calvin Klein, on September 21, 1996. Life as a Kennedy, and the public scrutiny that came with it, proved stressful for Bessette. The fashion police named her a trendsetter and compared her to a young Jackie. Gossip columns speculated on just when the newlyweds planned to start a family. She tried to keep a low profile but paparazzi followed her and John everywhere—and recorded every public spat. Carolyn's way of dealing with the media—not speaking and trying to blend into the background—made her come off as cold and aloof.

In 1999, the tabloids reported that the latest source of friction between John and Carolyn was his new passion for piloting. Insiders claimed she disapproved and refused to go up with him. But John disputed the stories, claiming she enjoyed flying with him in his Piper Saratoga as much as he enjoyed piloting it. Flying was a hobby friends say Jackie had strongly discouraged when she was alive, claiming she had a premonition he would be killed flying his own plane, just as Ari's son had been.

On July 16, 1999, John was flying his Piper to Martha's Vineyard to attend the wedding of his cousin Rory, the youngest of Robert Kennedy's eleven children. He was accompanied by Carolyn and her older sister Lauren, a venture capitalist. Although the weather report John looked at before takeoff indicated clear skies, the evening turned foggy and misty. Relatively inexperienced, Kennedy was not certified to fly by instrumentation. Experts believe he became disoriented in the haze. The plane crashed, killing John, Carolyn, and Lauren.

The Auchinclosses and Lee Radziwill

From childhood, Jackie's relationships with her mother and sister were complicated. Throughout her life, Jackie struggled to find common ground with Janet. On one hand, her mother represented a lifestyle Jackie found stifling—a career housewife whose primary function was to run the house and present the image of the perfect *Social Register* family. On the other hand, Jackie understood and embraced dedication to family. She also shared her mother's desire for deep financial security. Where they disconnected was in their views of a woman's place once the children were grown. Jackie was a teenager during World War II, when women entered the work force en masse and discovered independence and the fulfillment of having a career. Janet's goal was to be the perfect *Social Register* wife. Jackie saw her mother's pursuit of status as gauche. Like many daughters, Jackie loved her mother, but she didn't particularly like her. While her breeding demanded she treat her mother with respect, it didn't make her feel obligated to include her mother in every aspect of her life.

SHE SAID . . .

"I have made no provision in this my Will for my sister, Lee B. Radziwill, for whom I have great affection, because I have already done so during my lifetime. I do wish, however, to remember her children and . . . set aside the amount of Five Hundred Thousand Dollars for each child surviving me of my sister."

As children of a troubled marriage, Jackie and Lee developed a bunker mentality and forged a protective bond. But as they matured they also struggled with intense sibling rivalry. As teens, Lee—four years Jackie's junior—was always considered the more beautiful, the more precocious, and the more vivacious of the two. But Jackie had the sharper intellect and a playful, self-deprecating humor that drew people to her—and left Lee constantly overshadowed. Lee was also very insecure and took any slight teasing as a personal slight.

Auchinclosses

In November 1976, Jackie's stepfather Hughdie died at age seventy-nine after years of failing health. Life had thrown Hughdie unexpected hardships. Instead of enjoying his golden years, he spent the latter part of his life immersed in financial woes. He had lost the majority of his fortune through a series of bad investments. Although he kept his money problems a secret as much as he could from as many people as he could, his money crunch forced him to sell Merrywood.

> **FACT**
> Hughdie Auchincloss bought Merrywood in 1934 for $135,000. He spent an additional $100,000 in improvements. In 1962, he agreed to sell the property to a group of developers for $750,000. They planned to build three seventeen-story apartment buildings on the property. His attempt to sell the property to developers created a bitter community backlash.

After Hughdie's death, Jackie's mother, Janet, sold Hammersmith Farm, which became a private museum. Janet moved to a home in Georgetown. Jackie supported her mother by providing her with a million-dollar trust fund. But their relationship remained emotionally distant. Janet often appeared bitter at not being included in Jackie's life as much as she would have wanted. She passed away in 1989.

Lee Radziwill

Unlike Jackie, Lee showed little interest in proving herself as a career woman, channeling her energies instead on marrying well—and beating her sister to the altar. Her first marriage, to Michael

Canfield, took place on April 18, 1953, a month before Jack Kennedy proposed to Jackie. There were suggestions that Lee was jealous that Jackie had attracted the handsome young senator.

Separate Lives

During Jackie's time in the White House, Lee was one of her closest companions. By then Lee had divorced Canfield and remarried to Stas Radziwill. But after the assassination, the sisters' lives drifted in different directions. They always maintained a relationship but never got past their inherent resentment and competitiveness. It was Lee who first became romantically involved with Aristotle Onassis in 1963. But it was Jackie Ari married.

Where Jackie found fulfillment in being a wife and mother, Lee was on a constant search for her niche. In 1967, Lee appeared in a dinner theater production in Chicago of *Philadelphia Story*. Critics skewered Lee's performance, but the public wanted to see Jackie's sister and the play sold out. A year later, she starred in the television production of *Laura* on ABC. Again, the public watched in large numbers although her acting was universally panned by critics. Lee's close friend, Truman Capote, who had been instrumental in getting the TV movie produced, blamed Jackie for the critics' vitriol. He went on the David Suskind talk show and explained that the media came after Lee regardless of what she did because Jackie— then still seen as a grieving widow—was untouchable.

The Rift Deepens

Tension between the sisters flared in 1974 when Lee left Stas— after fourteen years of marriage and two children—and moved in with photographer Peter Beard. Jackie was close to her brother-in-law and let Lee know she disapproved of her actions. The estrangement was exacerbated the following year when, for reasons never publicly explained, Jackie prevented Lee from attending Aristotle Onassis's funeral. Lee reacted bitterly, but the resentment went much deeper. Lee's life seemed in constant upheaval and turmoil while Jackie flourished in her new, post-Onassis life. When Lee heard Jackie had been offered an editor's job at Viking, she took out her frustration on Tom Guinzburg when she ran into him at a dinner party.

Through it all, Jackie still felt responsible for the care of her younger sister. Lee was usually in dire need of money and Jackie frequently helped her out financially, but the emotional bond between them was forever damaged.

The Kennedy Mystique

Despite the tension that her marriage to Onassis caused, Jackie was always considered a Kennedy first. After taking her editing job, she saw less of the family but remained closely invested. She showed her affection through gifts and notes. Every year Jackie hosted a Labor Day weekend beach barbecue for the Kennedy family near Red Gate Farm.

Senator Edward Kennedy, Jacqueline Kennedy Onassis, John F. Kennedy Jr., Caroline Kennedy Schlossberg, and Edwin Schlossberg at an award ceremony, 1992

Photo Credit: Herb Swanson/AFP/Getty Images

As always, Jackie showed special attentiveness to Rose Kennedy, visiting her in Hyannis Port. When Rose was still able, they would go for walks on the beach. Later, when her health declined, Jackie sat by her and just kept her company for an afternoon. Jackie also became close to Joan Kennedy after her divorce from Ted. Through Jackie, Joan's book, *The Joy of Classical Music: A Guide for You and Your Family* was published by Doubleday. They shared a common bond of children, marriages played out in the public spotlight, and being Kennedys.

Not only were the Kennedys successful, they were attractive. Jackie, Jack, and their young children were one of the most photogenic First Families in history. The entire Kennedy clan exuded vigor and health. Likewise, Jackie kept herself in good physical shape with regular exercise and a careful diet.

THEY SAID...

"As a mother, she was selflessly devoted to her children and never wavered in the value she placed on being a mother. . . . She was a great support to me, personally . . . about how she had managed so well to carve out the space and privacy that children need to grow into what they have a right to become."

—Hillary Rodham Clinton

Tall, slender, and finely muscled, John Jr. was a chip off the Kennedy block from the time he was a teenager. Caroline, however, sometimes struggled with her weight as a teen and young adult. According to one anecdote, Jackie once canceled Caroline's credit card after seeing she had purchased two pounds of barbecue spareribs at Mr. Chow. She only reinstated the card after Caroline agreed to start jogging around the Central Park Reservoir with her mom.

The Kennedy mystique as embodied by Jackie went beyond achievement and physical attractiveness—it was breeding and charisma. When she walked into a room, Jackie commanded attention. People wanted to bask in her presence. Jackie had the ability to make whomever she was talking to feel as if they were the only person in the room. She was also unfailingly polite and raised her children to be equally courteous. Although Jackie enjoyed fine things such as art and antiques, she was also unpretentious and made sure John and Caroline did not grow up spoiled little rich kids. For example, unlike some Upper East Side scions, they never had private cars drive them to school—they took the bus or subway.

THEY SAID...

"My mother parented for two. She was deliberate in ensuring that my father's interests and concerns were part of our upbringing— and some of her own, too, which were not his. . . . She took a lot of pride in being a good mother. I'm glad people think it worked."

—John F. Kennedy Jr.

The well-chronicled Kennedy ambition has always been tempered by a commitment to public service and philanthropy. Jackie instilled those values in her children. As adults, both Caroline and John devoted time and money—sometimes anonymously—to a number of causes. Caroline helped raise $65 million for New York's public schools. In his twenties, John founded Reaching Up, a program that improved the quality of care for the mentally disabled by provided training for front-line health care workers.

Chapter 17

A LIFE WELL LIVED

When she died, Jacqueline Bouvier Kennedy Onassis was arguably the most famous woman of the twentieth century. The shy, awkward debutante had matured into a woman of substance. By the end of her life she had come full circle. After being adored as America's First Widow and scorned as a perceived gold digger during her marriage to Onassis, she was finally embraced as an icon who lived life on her own terms. More than anything, Jackie's fierce individuality shaped her enduring legacy.

Later Years

From the time Maurice moved into 1040, Jackie lived a quiet, ful-filled life. At Doubleday, she pursued book projects and writers with a finely honed literary passion. She reveled in her children and grandchildren and spent time in Central Park, jogging every morning around the reservoir and taking walks in the afternoons and early evenings, either alone or with Maurice. Summers were spent on Martha's Vineyard. Although Jackie shied away from social events, she frequently entertained her circle of friends at her Upper East Side apartment. And she continued to devote time and money to pet causes.

THEY SAID...

"Going back to our childhood days, she always loved New York and everything about it—the museums, the parks, the people. . . . She was always drawn back to New York. She chose to bring up her children in the city. She got into publishing because she knew it would be an educational experience—she would learn some-thing every moment."

—Nancy Tuckerman

To her friends and associates, these years were among her happiest and most contented. She found her continued notori-ety bemusing but had come to terms with it. As always, John and Caroline were her primary concern. While she might nudge, she never pushed, contrary to tabloid speculation that Jackie forbade her son from pursuing an acting career after he appeared in several theater productions. John, though, stated publicly that it was always just a diversion for him, not a vocation.

President Bill Clinton, Senator Edward Kennedy, and Jacqueline Kennedy Onassis chat together, 1993

Photo Credit: Dirck Halstead/Time & Life Pictures/Getty Images

Sudden Illness

In June 1993, Jackie and Maurice took a trip to France. Jackie came down with a summer cold that left her exhausted, and they flew back home to spend the rest of the summer on Martha's Vineyard. When Jackie returned to work at Doubleday in September, she had yet to shake what she believed was a lingering cold. Her children suggested she cut back on her schedule to give herself a chance to recuperate. Instead, she spent weekends riding in the country, participating in hunts. During a ride in November, Jackie fell off her horse. She was knocked briefly unconscious and taken to the hospital. During the examination, doctors noticed she had a swollen lymph node in her groin. She felt better after taking a course of antibiotics, but she still wasn't at full strength. When she returned to New York, she still felt weak enough to cancel several business appointments.

SHE SAID . . .

"I feel it is a kind of hubris. I have always been proud of keeping so fit. I swim, and I jog, and I do my push-ups, and walk around the reservoir, and I gave up smoking 40 years ago—and now this suddenly happens."

Her physical malaise lasted though the Christmas season, although her spirits were high. She decorated her apartment with a tree and took Rose for her first trip to the ballet. She and Maurice left for a Caribbean cruise during Christmas week. But the trip was cut short after Jackie developed severe back and abdominal pain. She also discovered a second swollen lymph node, this one in her neck. Back in New York she was admitted to New York Hospital-Cornell Medical Center for a series of tests. The results were sobering: Jackie was diagnosed with non-Hodgkin's lymphoma.

QUESTION
What is non-Hodgkin's lymphoma?
Non-Hodgkin's lymphoma, or NHL, is a cancer of the immune system. Typical symptoms include enlarged lymph nodes, fever, and weight loss. There are many different types of lymphoma, and the causes are complex and largely unknown. Prognosis and treatment depend on the stage and type of disease. Nearly 20,000 Americans die from NHL annually.

Jackie's doctors recommended she undergo aggressive chemotherapy. She endured the treatment without complaint, assuring everyone it wasn't unbearable. The good part was that she could read a book while the chemo was administered. Despite her condition, Jackie remained upbeat, cheerful, and optimistic. Some friends wondered if she wasn't putting on a front to protect her friends and family from the gravity of the situation.

Jackie's illness was made public in February 1994, prompting an outpouring of well wishes from acquaintances and strangers alike. Initially, her prognosis was hopeful—doctors told her there was a fifty-fifty chance the chemotherapy would stabilize her form of NHL.

> **THEY SAID...**
>
> "I knew she was very ill, and I knew she wasn't going to live long. I left her one of my garden books, and I ended my note by saying: Let's go hunting together next year. She sent me a handwritten note back that said: 'Wouldn't it be fun? Let's do it.'"
>
> —C. Z. Guest

Final Days

For a while it seemed Jackie would conquer cancer in the same way she had overcome all the other obstacles and challenges in her life. During her treatment, Maurice became her constant companion. He tended to her at home and accompanied her on walks through her beloved Central Park. In April, they were photographed strolling through the park on a warm spring afternoon. The scarf and trench coat she wore contrasted starkly with the shirtsleeves worn by others in the shot. Although thinner than usual, Jackie appeared alert and animated.

On April 14, Jackie's health took a sudden, dramatic downward turn. She collapsed at home and was rushed to the hospital where doctors repaired bleeding ulcers, a complication from her chemotherapy. Doctors also discovered the cancer had spread to her lungs. Within weeks Jackie began suffering terrible pain in her legs and arms. She also went through moments of confusion, a sign the disease had now spread to her brain. She went back to the hospital yet again, this time so doctors could insert a tube into her brain to relieve pressure and to administer drugs.

The cancer kept spreading. Before long her speech and gait were affected. On the evening of May 15, Jackie developed an excruciating headache. Maurice checked her into New York Hospital, where she was treated for pneumonia. Doctors also performed another scan, which showed the cancer had moved into her liver and she was experiencing kidney failure.

There was nothing medical science could do for her except prolong the inevitable. Jackie faced death the same way she had lived life: on her own terms. She refused any more treatment and went home to spend her final days with John, Caroline, and Maurice by her side day and night.

Nancy Tuckerman, acting as official family spokesperson, announced that Jackie's cancer had progressed and that she would not seek any further treatment because it would be futile. Jackie also refused antibiotics for her pneumonia. Jackie was dying; the only question was when the end would come.

As the street in front of her building filled with strangers holding a silent, respectful vigil, her closest friends were summoned to 1040 for a final farewell. Ted Kennedy flew to New York, as did other family members. Jackie arranged for her priest, Monsignor George Bardes of St. Thomas More Church, to administer last rites while she was still conscious. He also her heard her final confession. Soon afterward, she slipped into a coma.

> **FACT**
>
> The sacrament of Last Rites is a Catholic ritual for the dying. It is administered in three steps: first, the priest hears the person's last confession. Next he performs the Anointing of the Sick. Last is Viaticum—final Communion. *Viaticum* is the Latin word for "provision for the journey."

At approximately 10:15 P.M. on May 19, 1994, Jacqueline Bouvier Kennedy Onassis died. Her children and Maurice were at her bedside. John Jr. reported she passed on "surrounded by her friends and her family and her books, and the people and things that she loved."

Funeral and Burial

Jackie spent the majority of her life fighting for privacy.

SHE SAID . . .

"I'm almost glad it [the cancer] happened because it's given me a second life. I laugh and enjoy things so much more. . . . But even if I only have five years left, so what? I've had a great run."

But Caroline and John understood their mother's place in history, so they orchestrated a funeral and burial that was both public and private. It gave those closest to her the intimacy they needed to grieve and simultaneously allowed Americans everywhere a chance to pay tribute.

Maria Porfido holds a copy of the *New York Post* as she stands outside Jacqueline Kennedy Onassis's New York City apartment

Photo Credit: Timothy Clary/AFP/Getty Images

St. Ignatius Loyola Church

The funeral took place in New York at St. Ignatius Loyola Church, the same church where Jackie had been baptized and confirmed. Somber spectators began arriving before dawn. By the time the hearse arrived, thousands had gathered outside, the crowd covering three city blocks. Some knelt in prayer, others cried as attendants opened the back of the hearse and removed the mahogany casket, covered with ferns and a cross made from white lilies of the valley.

One thousand people packed the church for the ninety-minute service. Many were next-generation Kennedys including Robert F. Kennedy Jr., Timothy Shriver, Christopher Lawford, William Kennedy Smith, and Edward Kennedy Jr. Others were family friends such as Pierre Salinger, Dave Powers, and Roosevelt Grier. John Jr.'s then-longtime girlfriend, actress Daryl Hannah, and Maria Shriver's husband, action film star Arnold Schwarzenegger represented Hollywood. Fellow First Ladies Hillary Rodham Clinton and Lady Bird Johnson also came to pay respects to their friend and colleague. The ceremony also featured opera singer Jessye Norman performing *Ave Maria*.

John Jr. told the congregation that he and Caroline had struggled to find a reading that properly captured Jackie's essence, which, he said, could be summed up by three qualities: "the love of words, the bonds of home and family, and her spirit of adventure." He then read a passage from the Book of Isaiah. Caroline reminisced about her mother's love for

SHE SAID . . .

"When you get written about a lot, you just think of it as a little cartoon that runs along the bottom of your life—but one that doesn't have much to do with your life. . . . The sensational pieces will continue to appear as long as there is a market for them. One's real life is lived on another private level."

Martha's Vineyard before reading Edna St. Vincent Millay's "Cape Cod." Maurice Tempelsman recited another poem, "Ithaka," by C. P. Cavafy. He ended with his own words: "And now the journey is over, too short, alas, too short. It was filled with adventure and wisdom, laughter and love, gallantry and grace. So farewell, farewell."

Senator Ted Kennedy delivered the eulogy but somewhat pointedly did not mention her marriage to Onassis. Instead, he focused on Jackie's dedication to her family and country.

THEY SAID...

"And then, during those four endless days in 1963, she held us together as a family and a country. In large part because of her, we could grieve and then go on. She lifted us up, and in the doubt and darkness, she gave her fellow citizens back their pride as Americans. She was then thirty-four years old. . . . She graced our history. And for those of us who knew and loved her—she graced our lives."

—Senator Ted Kennedy

Arlington

After the funeral ceremony, Caroline, John, and Maurice led an intimate group of Jackie's closest friends and family to Washington for the burial. It was her wish to be buried next to John F. Kennedy and their two children, Arabella and Patrick, in Arlington National Cemetery.

President Clinton met the family's chartered jet at National Airport and led a twenty-eight-car motorcade. It was a clear, hot day but thousands of spectators stood along the route to Arlington to pay their respects.

The brief graveside ceremony was conducted by the Reverend Philip J. Hannan, retired Roman Catholic Archbishop of New

Orleans. As auxiliary bishop of Washington in 1963, he had presided over John F. Kennedy's funeral. As the ceremony ended, the bells of Washington's National Cathedral tolled sixty-four times—once for each year of Jackie's life. Only 100 people were invited to the ceremony, but Caroline and John allowed television cameras to film from a distance and millions of Americans tuned in to watch Jackie be laid to rest next to the man who had been the love of her life. As the mourners walked away, Caroline placed a long-stemmed white flower on her mother's coffin. John knelt to kiss it before touching the black granite marker on his father's adjacent grave. They both visited the grave of their uncle, Senator Robert F. Kennedy, and said a silent prayer before leaving.

Caroline Kennedy Schlossberg and John F. Kennedy Jr. at graveside ceremonies for Jacqueline Kennedy Onassis

Photo Credit: David Ake/AFP/Getty Images

Memorials

The normally jaded and cynical New York press showed uncharacteristic respect and deference in the wake of Jackie's death. Few others had ever embodied the vibrancy and the appeal of the city as Jackie had. She represented the best New York had to offer: creativity, intellectualism, social awareness, and advocacy, all pursued with a unique and inimitable style.

After Jackie's death, there was a renewed interest and appreciation in her life and in her historical, political, and social impact. In the days, weeks, and months following her death, tributes to Jackie poured in from every corner of society, and memorials in her honor continued for years after. Central Park's main reservoir was renamed the Jacqueline Kennedy Onassis Reservoir. A residence hall at the George Washington University was renamed Jacqueline Bouvier Kennedy Onassis Hall. New York's Jacqueline Kennedy Onassis High School for International Careers in midtown Manhattan was dedicated by the city in 1995. It is the only high school in America named in her honor. In a 1999 Gallup poll, Americans named Jackie among the list of widely admired people of the twentieth century.

Legacy

On the day of Jackie's funeral, the country mourned not just the passing of an individual but everything Jacqueline Kennedy Onassis represented. She established a standard of social awareness and activism that current First Ladies strive to match. She became a symbol of American grit and grace in the days, weeks, and years following her husband's assassination. In her, Americans saw their own lives; the same complex tapestry of joy, tragedy, triumph, and heartache that everyone experiences—except Jackie's played out in public. Her unwavering independence and her courage to live life on her own terms occasionally earned both criticism and grudging respect.

Today Jackie is remembered as both a woman of her time and ahead of it. She is honored as an enduring icon who continues to inspire new generations of women to believe that it is possible to balance family, career, and social activism. Her most admirable legacy is her commitment to staying true to herself. That was the key to a life well lived.

Jacqueline Kennedy Onassis

Photo Credit: David McGough/Time & Life Pictures/Getty Images

Appendix A

TIMELINE

1929 Born in Southampton, Long Island on July 28

1933 Sister Caroline Lee born March 3

1938 Wins Blue Ribbon at East Hampton Horse Show

1940 Parents divorce

1942 Mother marries Hugh Auchincloss;
Jackie goes to live at Merrywood

1944 Enrolls at Miss Porter's School

1947 Named Debutante of the Year; enrolls at Vassar

1948 Makes first trip to Europe

1949 Attends the Sorbonne for a year as an exchange student

1951 Graduates from George Washington University

1951 Wins *Vogue*'s Prix de Paris writing contest;
introduced to Congressman John Kennedy

1952 Announces engagement to John Husted in
January; breaks off engagement in March

1952 Is assigned to be Inquiring Camera Girl
at *Washington Times-Herald*

1953 Announces engagement to John F. Kennedy
on June 23; marries on September 12

1957 Father, John "Black Jack" Bouvier, dies August 3

1957 Daughter Caroline Bouvier Kennedy born November 27

1960 Kennedy defeats Nixon making Jackie First Lady
elect; son John Jr. born November 25

1961 Kennedy inauguration on January 20 makes
Jackie third-youngest First Lady

1961 Announces White House restoration plans February 23

1962 Hosts televised tour of the White House on February 14

1962 Meets with Pope Paul XXIII in Rome on March 11

1963 Gives birth to son Patrick Bouvier on August 7,
who dies two days later

1963 John F. Kennedy assassinated on November 22

1964 Moves to New York with children

1968 Robert Kennedy assassinated on June 6

1968 Marries Aristotle Onassis

1975 Joins in fight to save Grand Central Station

1975 Onassis dies March 15

1976 Is hired at Viking Press as book editor

1978 Moves to Doubleday as associate editor

1979 John F. Kennedy Library and Museum in Boston
dedicated October 20

1982 Maurice Tempelsman moves into 1040

1988 Becomes grandmother for first time to Caroline's daughter
Rose Kennedy Schlossberg

1994 Dies May 19 in New York City; buried next to JFK
in Arlington four days later

Appendix B

WHO'S WHO: AN A–Z DIRECTORY OF THE PEOPLE IN JACKIE'S LIFE

Auchincloss, Hugh D.: stepfather (d. 1976)

Auchincloss, Hugh D. "Yusha" III: stepbrother

Auchincloss, James: half brother

Bartlett, Charlie and Martha: friends who introduced her to Jack Kennedy

Beale, Edith Ewing (née Bouvier): paternal aunt (d. 1977)

Bessette, Carolyn: daughter-in-law (d. 1999)

Bouvier, Caroline Lee: sister. Married to Michael Canfield, Stanislaw Radziwill, and Herbert Ross

Bouvier, Caroline (née Ewing): paternal great-grandmother (d. 1929)

Bouvier, John Vernou: paternal great-grandfather (d. 1926)

Bouvier, John Vernou II: paternal grandfather (d. 1948)

Bouvier, John "Black Jack" Vernou III: father (d. 1957)

Bouvier, Maude Frances (née Sergeant): paternal grandmother (d. 1940)

Bowdoin, Helen and Judy: sisters who accompanied Jackie on her first trip to Europe

Cassini, Oleg: favorite designer (d. 2006)

Danseuse: favorite horse

de Renty, Countess Guyot: Parisian host during her year studying at the Sorbonne

Gallagher, Mary: personal secretary

Gates, John "Demi": friend

Gilpatrick, Ros: boyfriend c. 1968

Husted, John: fiancé (January–March 1952)

Kennedy, Arabella: daughter (d. 1956)

Kennedy, John Fitzgerald: husband (1953–63)

Kennedy, John Fitzgerald Jr: son (d. 1999)

Kennedy, Joseph: father-in-law (d. 1969)

Kennedy, Robert: brother-in-law (d. 1968)

Kennedy, Rose: mother-in-law (d. 1995)

Kennedy, Patrick Bouvier: son (d. 1963)

Manchester, William: author who wrote book about JFK's assassination

Morris, Janet Norton Bouvier Auchincloss (née Lee): mother (d. 1989)

Lee, James Thomas: maternal grandfather (d. 1968)

Lee, Margaret (née Merritt): maternal grandmother (d. 1943)

Lincoln, Evelyn: JFK's secretary

Lowe, Ann: designer who made Jackie's wedding dress

Morris, Bingham "Booch": stepfather

Onassis, Alexander: stepson (d. 1973)

Onassis, Aristotle: second husband (d. 1975)

Onassis, Christina: stepdaughter (d. 1988)

Paredes, Providencia: personal attendant

Pei, I. M.: architect picked to design JFK library

Rutherfurd, Janet Jennings (née Auchincloss): half sister (d. 1985)

Sargent, John: friend who hired her at Doubleday

Schlossberg, Caroline Bouvier (née Kennedy): daughter

Shriver, Sargent: brother-in-law and political activist

Tempelsman, Maurice: live-in companion from mid-1970s to JKO's death

Tuckerman, Nancy: best friend

Turnure, Pam: worked in Jackie's NY office

Vidal, Gore: Hughdie's stepson

Waldrop, Frank: editor of the *Washington Times-Herald*

Warnecke, Jack: boyfriend in the early 1970s

Appendix C

A GEOGRAPHICAL TOUR OF JACKIE'S LIFE

1040 Fifth Avenue: Jackie's Upper East Side apartment

Bethesda, Maryland: site of Holton Arms School, where Jackie attended grammar school and first year of high school between 1942 and 1944

Central Park: Manhattan's public park

East Hampton, Long Island: resort community where Bouvier summer home Lasata was located

Georgetown, Washington, D.C.: lived with JFK in house on N Street

Hammersmith Farm: Auchincloss estate in Newport, Rhode Island

Hyannis Port: resort village on Cape Cod, Massachusetts, where Kennedy compound is located

Lasata: the Bouvier family summer home in East Hampton

Most Holy Trinity Catholic Cemetery: East Hampton, Long Island, cemetery where Jackie's father and other Bouvier relatives are buried

Merrywood: Auchincloss family home located in McLean, Virginia

Newport, Rhode Island: summer resort city; Jackie and JFK were married in Newport's St. Mary's Church

Palm Beach, Florida: resort city; site of Kennedy family vacation home

Paris, France: where Jackie attended the Sorbonne from 1949 to 1950

Poughkeepsie, New York: site of Vassar College

Skorpios: Aegean island owned by Aristotle Onassis; where she married the Greek tycoon and they lived

Washington, D.C.: attended George Washington University 1950–51; lived in White House 1961–63

Appendix D
TO FIND OUT MORE

Books

Abbott, James A. *A Frenchman in Camelot: The Decoration of the Kennedy White House by Stéphane Boudin.* Garrison, NY: Boscobel Restoration Inc., 1995.

Abbott, James A., and Elaine M. Rice. *Designing Camelot: The Kennedy White House Restoration.* New York: Van Nostrand-Reinhold, 1998.

Anderson, Christopher P. *Jack and Jackie: Portrait of an American Marriage.* New York: Avon 1997.

Anderson, Christopher P. *Jackie after Jack: Portrait of the Lady.* New York: Morrow, 1999.

Anthony, Carl Sferrazza. *As We Remember Her: Jacqueline Kennedy Onassis in the Words of Her Family and Friends.* New York: Perigee Trade, 1997.

Anthony, Carl Sferrazza. *Kennedy White House: Family Life and Pictures, 1961–1963.* New York: Simon & Schuster, 2001.

Baldrige, Letitia. *In the Kennedy Style: Magical Evenings in the Kennedy White House.* New York: Doubleday, 1998.

Bowles, Hamish, Rachael Lambert Mellon, Arthur M. Schlesinger, and New York Metropolitan Museum of Art. *Jacqueline Kennedy: The White House Years: Selections from the John F. Kennedy Library and Museum.* New York: Bulfinch Press, 2001.

Bradford, Sarah. *America's Queen: A Life of Jacqueline Kennedy Onassis.* New York: Viking Press, 2000.

Branch, Shelley, and Sue Callaway. *What Would Jackie Do? An Inspired Guide to Distinctive Living.* New York: Gotham Books, 2006.

Cassini, Oleg. *A Thousand Days of Magic: Dressing the First Lady for the White House.* New York: Rizzoli International Publications, 1995.

Davis, John H. *Jacqueline Bouvier: An Intimate Memoir.* Hoboken, New Jersey: Wiley, 1998.

Flaherty, Tina Santi. *What Jackie Taught Us: Lessons from the Remarkable Life of Jacqueline Kennedy Onassis.* New York: Perigee Trade, 2005.

Garside, Anne, and Orlando Suero, photographer. *Camelot at Dawn: Jacqueline and John Kennedy in Georgetown, May, 1954.* Baltimore: Johns Hopkins University Press, 2001.

Heymann, David C. *A Woman Named Jackie: An Intimate Biography of Jacqueline Bouvier Kennedy Onassis.* New York: Kensington, 1989.

Kelleher, K. L. *Jackie: Beyond the Myth of Camelot.* Tinicum, PA: Xlibris, 2001.

Kennedy, Caroline, ed. *The Best-Loved Poems of Jacqueline Kennedy Onassis.* New York: Hyperion, 2001.

Keogh, Pamela Clarke. *Jackiestyle.* New York: HarperCollins Publishers, 2001.

Klein, Edward. *All Too Human: The Love Story of Jack and Jackie Kennedy.* New York: St. Martin's Press, 2003.

Klein, Edward. *Farewell, Jackie: A Portrait of Her Final Days.* New York: Viking Books, 2004.

Klein, Edward. *Just Jackie: Her Private Years.* New York: Ballantine Books, 1999.

Klein, Edward. *The Kennedy Curse: Why Tragedy Has Haunted America's First Family for 150 Years*. New York: Pocket Books, 1996.

Koestenbaum, Wayne. *Jackie under My Skin: Interpreting an Icon*. Waterville, ME: Thorndike, 1995.

Leaming, Barbara. *Mrs. Kennedy: The Missing History of the Kennedy Years*. New York: Free Press, 2001.

Lowe, Jacques. *Camelot: The Kennedy Years*. Kansas City, MO: Andrews McMeel Publishing, 1996.

Manchester, William. *The Death of a President*. New York: Harper & Row Publishers, 1967.

Mars, Julie. *Jackie*, gift edition. Kansas City, MO: Andrews McMeel, Ariel Books, 1996.

Moutsatsos, Kiki Feroudi. *The Onassis Women: An Eyewitness Account*. New York: Berkley, 1998.

Mulvaney, Jay. *Jackie: The Clothes of Camelot*. New York: St. Martin's Press, 2001.

Pottker, Jan. *Janet and Jackie: The Story of a Mother and Her Daughter, Jacqueline Kennedy Onassis*. New York: St. Martin's Griffin, 2001.

Radziwill, Lee. *Happy Times*. New York: Assouline, 2001.

Sgubin, Marta, and Nancy Nicholas. *Cooking for Madam: Recipes and Reminiscences from the Home of Jacqueline Kennedy Onassis*. New York: Scribners, 1998.

Spada, James. *Jackie: Her Life in Pictures*. New York: St. Martin's Press, 2000.

Spoto, Donald. *Jacqueline Bouvier Kennedy Onassis: A Life*. New York: St. Martin's Press, 2000.

Taraborrelli, J. Randy. *Jackie, Ethel, Joan: The Women of Camelot*. New York: Warner Books, 2000.

West, J. B., with Mary Lynn Kotz. *Upstairs at the White House: My Life with the First Ladies.* New York: Coward, McCann & Geoghegan, 1973.

West, Naomi, and Catherine Wilson. *Jackie.* New York: MQ Publications, 2006.

White House Historical Association. *The White House: An Historic Guide.* Washington, DC: White House Historical Association and the National Geographic Society, 2001.

Wolff, Perry. *A Tour of the White House with Mrs. John F. Kennedy.* New York: Doubleday & Company, 1962.

Catalog

Exhibition Catalogue, Sale 6834: The Estate of Jacqueline Kennedy Onassis April 23–26, 1996. Sothebys, Inc., 1996.

Collections

John F. Kennedy Library; Boston, Massachusetts

Jacqueline Kennedy Onassis Clipping Files: The largest and most complete clipping file on Jacqueline Kennedy Onassis. Two boxes of a wide variety of American and European newspaper and magazine clippings, and some ephemera, related to Jacqueline Bouvier Kennedy Onassis, from 1953 to 1994. Many pieces have no date or publication.

Papers of Jacqueline Bouvier Kennedy Onassis, 1930s–1993: These papers are currently closed.

Papers of Jacqueline Bouvier Kennedy Onassis, 1951. Jacqueline Bouvier's Prix de Paris entry is "open in part."

Papers of Jacqueline Bouvier Kennedy Onassis, Condolences 1963–1968. 16 feet. This lengthy collection of condolence letters concerning the death of President Kennedy is open.

Papers of Jacqueline Bouvier Kennedy Onassis, Condolences 1994. This collection of condolence letters sent to the family upon Jacqueline Onassis's death is open.

Oral History Collection. The Kennedy Presidential Library has a copy of the oral interview of Jacqueline Kennedy done by the Lyndon Baines Johnson Presidential Library.

Web Sites

The White House, Biography of Jacqueline Kennedy
www.whitehouse.gov/history/firstladies/jk35.html

Arlington National Cemetery, Jacqueline Bouvier Kennedy Onassis
www.whitehouse.gov/history/firstladies/jk35.html

Court TV, The Will of Jacqueline Kennedy Onassis
www.courttv.com/archive/legaldocs/newsmakers/wills/onassis.html

USAToday.com, Jacqueline Kennedy Onassis Estate sale Index
www.usatoday.com/life/special/jackie/ljack000.htm

Plays and Stage Productions about Jackie

- *Jackie-O* an opera by Michael Daugherty
- *JACKS* by Lys Anzia
- *Cirque Jacqueline* by Andrea Reese
- *Jackie, An American Life* by Gip Hoppe
- *Jackie Undressed* by Andree Stolte
- *The Secret Letters of Jackie & Marilyn* by Mark Hampton and Michael Sharp, O'Reilly Theatre, Pittsburgh, PA.
- *The First Lady* by Herman van Veen and Lori Spee

Songs about Jackie

- "Jackie Will Save Me" by American rock band Shiny Toy Guns
- "Jackie's Strength" by Tori Amos
- "Tire Me" by Rage Against the Machine
- "Jacqueline/Jackie-O" by Strung Out
- "Don't Let Me Explode" by The Hold Steady

Appendix E
MEMORIAL TRIBUTES

On June 29, 1994, the Senate resolved to print an official collection of statements made in honor of the former First Lady. It passed without objection. It included tributes from more than fifty senators and representatives, many of whom knew her well and mourned her as a friend. The following are excerpts from some of their remarks.

George J. Mitchell, Senate Majority Leader

"Mrs. Onassis never asked to be a legend. But once she was thrust into the national and international spotlight, it was something she could not avoid. She conducted herself with grace and dignity that others could only emulate. Her contributions to the cultural heritage of this Nation are numerous, and we, as Americans, owe her a tremendous debt of gratitude."

Senator Joseph R. Biden Jr. of Delaware

"Mr. President, as the Nation mourned, and continues to mourn, the death of Jacqueline Bouvier Kennedy Onassis, many of us have tried, in private and public reflections, to define and explain her enduring place in our common history and our shared consciousness. It is a difficult, if not an impossible task, as it always is when we try to put into words the meaning of a life that has touched our very spirit and left us forever changed. It never was the ambition of the woman we knew, and will always remember, as 'Jackie' to have the kind of fundamental public influence. It was a part of her style that she did not cherish celebrity, a part of her grace that she did not succumb to its temptations, and a part of her dignity that she did not surrender to fame, but sought—in the end, it seemed, successfully—to make peace with it on her own terms."

Representative Lucien E. Blackwell of Pennsylvania

"I did not know her. But, I believe she knew me. We never met. From a distance, however, the force of her personality and what she stood for made her seem near. . . .

"When she was First Lady, at the tender age of thirty-one, she had ascended to the top of the ladder. Many, too many, in America remained on the lower rungs. Hers was the language of lyrics, theirs more common. She knew what America and the World offered. They didn't even dream about what she knew. In public, she dressed smartly. They just dressed smart, depending on the weather. Nonetheless, there were few who were not warmed by the thought and feeling that she was First Lady to all America. . . .

"They believed the First Lady could see what they saw, could feel what they felt, understood what they understood. Jacqueline Bouvier Kennedy Onassis. I did not know her. But, she knew us. She was a First Lady, with class."

Senator Russell D. Feingold of Wisconsin

"We grieved for Mrs. Onassis . . . because she reminded us of a time when we were more sure of ourselves and of our place in the world. When she burst onto the American scene in the late 1950s and early 1960s it seemed as though people had more faith, not just in themselves but also in their Federal Government."

Representative Benjamin A. Gilman of New York

"Today, our young people may not appreciate that, prior to the Kennedy administration, the White House was considered a temporary residence by its occupants, and enjoyed little historic significance.

"Mrs. Kennedy, virtually single-handedly, transformed the White House into a national treasure. She scoured the Nation for furnishings and trappings of by-gone eras, and in many cases through cajolery, convinced private citizens to re-donate to the American people items of historic significance. As a result of her crusade, the White House became an invaluable historic landmark during her husband's administration. As hard as it may be to believe today, prior to Jackie Kennedy's tenure as our First Lady the White House was not even officially listed by the Federal Government as a historic site. She vigorously campaigned for this designation, as she also vigorously campaigned for the funding—the vast majority of which was from the private sector—necessary for the restoration and preservation of the White House."

Senator John Glenn of Ohio

"I was privileged to first meet Jackie over thirty years ago, shortly after my orbital flight, when she and President Kennedy were in the White House. There were so many good times back then that it would be hard to recount all of them.

"Those who have described those years in the White House as Camelot surely know that a very large part of the reason was the style and the class and the elegance that Jackie brought to her duties as First Lady.

"Along with all other Americans who lived through that period in history, Annie and I stood literally in awe—utter awe—of the dignity, the grace, and the courage that she displayed in those sad and awful days following the President's assassination in Dallas."

Senator Howell Heflin of Alabama

"It is an understatement to say that America has never known— and will probably never know again—anyone else like Jacqueline Kennedy Onassis. When she died, people who had never met her spontaneously broke into tears, unable to explain exactly why. Perhaps it was because she was our last link to Camelot and all that it symbolized, a living symbol of an all-too-brief slice of the past during which anything seemed possible."

Senator Ernest F. Hollings of South Carolina

"As First Lady, Jackie Kennedy was not politically active on the model of Eleanor Roosevelt or Hillary Rodham Clinton. However, I dare say that she served the country more intensely and profoundly than any First Lady in history. She did so in the course of those dark days in November. At a time of unspeakable personal loss, when we should have been supporting and steadying her, it was she who supported and steadied us. It was a veiled and valiant Jackie Kennedy who supported and steadied an entire nation. For that act of sustained courage and fortitude, our beloved former First Lady will be remembered and honored for centuries to come."

Senator Kay Bailey Hutchison of Texas

"Madam President, I was just a college student during the Kennedy administration. Our generation of young women was profoundly affected by the grace and dignity of the First Lady. We were fascinated by her—as was the world."

Senator John Kerry of Massachusetts

"Whether or not we are aware, the image she defined of her husband—by characterizing his Presidency as Camelot—forever changed the standard for leaders in this country, and in fact, the world. She and her husband affected this period of history with enlightenment and idealism, making us all believe that collectively we were capable of great things, and making us more determined to pursue such potentials. Jackie set all of our sights a little higher."

Senator Carl Levin of Michigan

"She was a modern woman whose life in many ways personified the changing role of women in America during the second half of the twentieth century. Her interests were cultural, artistic, and many, and her good taste governed everything in which she involved herself. Protecting her children from the limelight that was forced upon her was probably the primary focus of her young life, and she raised them to be the fine young people they are today."

Representative Sander Levin of Michigan

"Mr. Speaker, the death of Jacqueline Kennedy Onassis evokes flashes of memory, first and foremost November 22 and its aftermath, her grace, her dignity, her strength.

"But as we watched television last night and this morning, my wife and I, there were also memories of those days before November 22, their excitement, their sense of decency, and their sense of the worthiness of public service. Some might call those memories illusion. I would call them hope.

"May that hope not pass on with Jackie Kennedy; instead, may it be rekindled."

Representative Jack Reed of Rhode Island

"When one stops and considers her life, we are struck with myriad images. I recall her interview with President Kennedy on Ed Morrow's *Person to Person*. She was a young woman whose soft-spoken grace and obvious love for her husband provided a spark of magic in the otherwise dreary routine of politics. I recall the extraordinary evening in the White House when she hosted Robert Frost, Igor Stravinsky, and Pablo Casals. She and her husband made the arts and culture fashionable not just in the salons of the privileged but throughout the land.

"Her life after the White House was full of accomplishments. She remained to her last day an image of grace and elegance. We mourn her passing and express our sincerest condolences to her family."

INDEX

Other titles ~~a~~ he
Everything® Profiles Series:

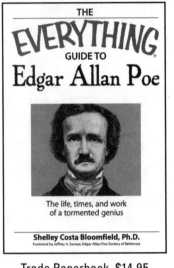

THE

EVERYTHING®
GUIDE TO
Edgar Allan Poe

The life, times, and work
of a tormented genius

Shelley Costa Bloomfield, Ph.D.
Foreword by Jeffrey A. Savoye, Edgar Allan Poe Society of Baltimore

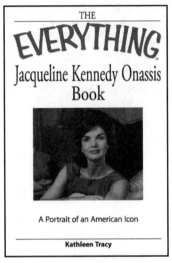

THE

EVERYTHING®
Jacqueline Kennedy Onassis
Book

A Portrait of an American Icon

Kathleen Tracy

Trade Paperback. $14.95
ISBN ~~10:~~ -530-4
ISBN 13 ~~978-1-598~~ 69-530-4

Trade Paperback, $14.95

EV~~ERYTHING~~
John~~~~

Relive the history, romance,
and tragedy of America's Camelot

Jessica McElrath

~~EVERYT~~HING®
~~Martin Luther~~ King Jr.

The Struggle. The Dream. The Legacy.

Jessica McElrath, The About.com Guide to African-American History
Foreword by Rev. Dale F. Andrews, Ph.D.

Trade Paperback, $14.95
ISBN 10: 1-59869-529-0
ISBN 13: 978-1-59869-529-8

Trade Paperback, $14.95
ISBN 10: 1-59869-528-2
ISBN 13: 978-1-59869-528-1

Available wherever books are sold!
Or call 1-800-258-0929 or visit *www. adamsmediastore.com.*